Crashing Into the Calm

Crashing Into the Calm

*A Memoir of Fourteen Missing Minutes
and Coming Back to Find Them*

JULIE BRITTAIN

TATE PUBLISHING
AND ENTERPRISES, LLC

Published by Tate Publishing & Enterprises, LLC
127 E. Trade Center Terrace | Mustang, Oklahoma 73064 USA
1.888.361.9473 | www.tatepublishing.com

Tate Publishing is committed to excellence in the publishing industry. The company reflects the philosophy established by the founders, based on Psalm 68:11,
"The Lord gave the word and great was the company of those who published it."

Book design copyright © 2015 by Tate Publishing, LLC. All rights reserved.
Cover design by Samson Lim
Interior design by Gram Telen
Cover painting by Paula Jones

Published in the United States of America
ISBN: 978-1-68028-057-9
Biography & Autobiography / Personal Memoirs
15.01.30

For my family
who never left my side.

For my friends
and everyone that
prayed for me.

For the doctors and nurses of St. Anthony's
Shawnee and Oklahoma City
for never giving up.

For anyone in search of themselves and their faith.

Contents

What I Knew "For Sure?"

I can do all things through Christ
who strengthens me.

—Philippians 4:13 (NKJV)

I once heard Oprah ask Johny Depp, "What do you know for sure?"

To tell you the truth, I thought I knew. I grew up watching Oprah. I never missed an episode. At the end of her interviews, she'd always ask her guests what they "knew for sure." Well, after so many years of watching her, I knew what mattered—to not give up on my dreams, the "secret," and definitely not to "sweat the small stuff."

After going through life and making mistakes, you believe that you have some sense of what was "not for sure," but did you know what was? I had a wonderful family and amazing friends. I felt like I'd lived and parented and worked my way to that exact moment when you realize "yes, I have it figured out!" That hasn't really happened yet. But at my age—thirty-eight—and living a pretty full life, so far I had come to the three "for sure" conclusions.

1. My laundry would *never* be done.

2. No matter how much my kids bickered, they did love each other.

3. And this one I just figured out—no matter what I *did*, my life was *never* going to change.

Well, I was wrong. Not about the laundry, but about my life. It did change.

My name is Julie Brittain. I am your typical wife and mother. I feel like I live the ever sought after American dream. I have a husband, Michael; three kids, Jordan, Raegan, and Bauer; a dog, Sparky; a house; and the wonderful crazy life that's balanced with work and a normal amount of mother's guilt. Every breath I've ever taken was for my children, and not just to yell at them. Most of the time, working meant you're worried about your kids and when you're with your kids or catching up at home, you're worried about your work.

As married parents, we live our lives in such a routine. That's what gives our chaos structure. You look up years later and your routine has turned into a rut and frustration is more normal to you than joy.

At least that's how it was for me. Until June 11, 2013. The day my twins', Jordan and Raegan, turned sixteen. Also, the night I died.

Let's Start at the Beginning

Therefore I tell you, do not be anxious about your life.

—Matthew 6:25 (ESV)

I remember being very little, probably about five or six. I'd flip my long brown hair and talk to myself in the big mirror by the front door. I'd walk over to the record player and I'd turn on the *Grease* album. I could dance and sing all day to those songs. "Summer Nights" and "Hopelessly Devoted to You" were my favorites. I had the little lines on the record memorized of where my favorite parts were so I could start and stop until I had every word memorized. I was the same way with the movie. I knew every word. I'd pause it and watch every scene over and over again. It wasn't any different the older I got. In the eighth grade, I went to see *When Harry Met Sally*. From that day on, it was my favorite movie. I probably watched it two thousand times. I still know every word.

Even when I was very young, I knew exactly what I wanted to do with my life. No one ever told me what to aspire to, I just knew. I remember making a list in my Hello Kitty notebook of all the things I wanted to do with my life. Most little girls dream of their wedding and having kids—not me. I wanted to write and act in movies, and live in Hollywood. I would make up my own characters and act them out in front of the mirror. I was different. At least I felt different.

Another way I was different was that I had asthma. I was the only person my age I knew with it too. Not easy. The first many years of my life, asthma inhalers had not been invented yet. You couldn't take breathing machines home. If I got sick, I had to go to the ER. I would try to go to the lake or run on the playground at school but I would always end up wheezing or not being able to breathe. When I did get that new blue Ventolin inhaler, it helped me have a more normal life. My friends, family, and teachers were always a huge help. My brother, Patrick, had asthma also so as a family we all learned how to deal with it. Eventually, we all got used to it. I had so many people always supporting and taking care of me.

I grew up in Shawnee, Oklahoma. I loved that it was a small town where everyone knew everyone. We all went to church and school together. Everyone believed in God and said the pledge of allegiance. A place where you could charge at the gas station and the pharmacy because they knew who you were. We rode our bikes in the neighborhood and knew to go home when the street lights came on.

Some of my fondest memories growing up were spending time at Steeple People and youth group with our church, St. Paul's.

Church camp, mission trips, middle school, and high school—we all went through our wild phases but remained close to our families and how we were raised.

Snow days were the best. We'd all stay the night at each other's houses and thaw out at the fireplace. I'd yell at my sister to leave us alone while my mom made her famous cookies, and my dad would yell at me to be nice to my sister. It sounds like a fairytale, yes, and it kind of was. I had a wonderful family and, to be honest, most people in this town were good people. I had the same group of friends my entire life. We rode bikes as kids and snuck out of the house as teenagers. In those days, we'd cruise Kickapoo and get cherry limeades at Sonic. We had our hearts broken and broke a few ourselves. We'd all been through a lot together. High school, college, weddings, kids—for the most part we all either stayed in touch or moved back to Shawnee to raise our families together. I did the Hollywood thing for years and decided it was time to come back. I wanted to live in Shawnee and be close to my family. My cousin Tracy and her husband, Steve, had six beautiful kids, and I wanted us all to raise our kids together and have big family Christmases. I wanted my kids to live in a town that cared about them. There's something great to be said about a town where you know *everyone*! My kids laugh about it and hate going to the grocery store because it takes so *long*. You have to allow at least thirty minutes for talking to everyone you see there. My closest friends live down the street and all of our kids are best friends. I'm that school mom that helps with fall carnival and Michael coaches baseball and football. Michael and I both worked in sales traveling the state and were home at night to run kids. We feel blessed to be a part of this community. I was in Junior Service League for ten years. Michael and his buddies run the youth sports in town and he helped coach high school sports for years too. Life was good. It was the life I never knew I wanted. I'd moved on from my wants and dreams of Hollywood and right into dance and soccer practices, and that was okay with me. I was happy. Even though I was happy, I still felt different.

My entire life, I had always felt different. Not better or worse, just different. I always wanted to do something really *great*. I wanted to do something that mattered. I had dreams—then they changed. Dreams change and life moves on. I wasn't resentful. I loved my husband and I lived for my kids. I just didn't want to completely lose myself, so…I kept writing. Writing was a way for me to stay creative, vent my emotions, and keep my hope for still doing something that really mattered. What I didn't realize is that I already was.

Six Degrees of Shawnee

Be watchful, stand firm in your faith, be courageous, be strong.
Let all that you do be done in love.

—1 Corinthians 16:13–14 (esv)

To truly understand my story, you have to understand the town I'm from—Shawnee, Oklahoma. It's a wonderful, smaller town that is truly like no other. It's like six degree of separation here. Everyone is connected. Either by marriage, divorce, family, kids—whatever it is, all are connected. There are many different groups of friends that hang out together in *town,* but everyone is friends with *each other.* Whether you went to high school together or are married to someone or have kids the same age might determine who your friends are, but everyone knows and likes each other. Here is my six degrees, my connections. This is not by any means the whole town or everyone I care about, but it will give you an idea of the people who are part of my story and just how linked together we all are. This is just to help you get to know them.

I'm Julie. I'm married to Michael Brittain. My parents are Mik and Betty Presley and I have a brother, Patrick, and a sister, Allyson. Pat is married to Carrie and they have Scout and Paxon. Allyson is married to Justin and they have Shelby. Michael's parents are Mike and Debi Brittain. He has three siblings—Jason, Kim, and Jennifer. Jason is with Meredith and his kids are Shaye and Tyler. Kim is married to Dennis and they have Dawson, Darrell, Kalyn, Kiera, and Klaira. Jennifer is married to Daniel and they have Brittain and Asa. We all went to high school together—different years of course—and our parents were friends before Michael and I were even dating.

Melisa is married to Chad. They have Gage and Creed. Chad's parents are Darryll and Pam. Melisa's parents, Phyllis and Jerry, are best friends with Richie and Donna Sue, who are Brooke's parents. Brooke and I have been friends since Grove Elementary. Angie is married to Ryan, whose best friend from Spiro married Danielle, who we've also known all of our lives and went to Grove with. Samantha and April C. were also Grovers and graduated with us. Kim is married to Chad S. who graduated with Melisa and is also friends with Michael and Chad and Ryan. Their other buddy is Jeff, who is married to Carol and they're also best friends with Terrie and Jason, who is also Melisa's brother. Carey is Chad's older brother who is married to April. They have Jordan and Cole. Cole dates Alex, who dances with us, and her mom is Jessica. Jeff and Carol have Elise and Jack. Terrie and Jason have Kaily and Bryce. Angie and Ryan have Logan, Kaylin, Teegan, and Casen. Kim and Chad have Kade.

All of our kids have all basically been raised together. We were all in Junior Service League, where I met Rachel and Summer. Summer is married to Brian and they have Kenzie and Langston. Langston and Bauer have been friends since they were in diapers and Michael has always coached them in sports. Rachel and Randy have Rebecca and Ryan, who goes to high school with all the kids and plays golf with Cole, April and Carey's son. April and Carey live on a ranch with horses and our friend Anne would go out there and ride horses. Anne used to be married to Greg and they had three girls—Catherine, Erin, and Alex. Greg was a doctor at the clinic and he remarried Jennifer, who was friends with Mary Kay whose husband is Dr. Holland and worked with Greg. Dr. Tony also works with them and he and his wife Heather and three girls lived across the street from us before we built a house just down the road. Two of Anne's girls, Erin and Alex, are twins and they are best friends with my twins since they met at three years old. Their other best buddies are Abby and Malory. Malory's mom and dad are Nancy and David, Abby's parents are Larry and Melanie. We met when the girls were in Pre-K at school. Melanie and Larry were a divorced couple who got along great. Everyone loves Melanie even though she hates Shawnee. It's kind of funny. Melanie was also very close to Anne-Holly-Terry and Tonya, whom I *love* as well. I used to walk with all of them at 5:00 a.m. every morning. Jana would walk with us too. Jana and Mike have two boys—Blake and Cade—and Blake played ball with Kim and Chad's son Kade. Anne was also buddies with Kristi, whose daughter Kelsey was Kaily's age and also good friends with Catherine. Kristi's sister is Sheryl and she was the principal at Grove. Patty is everyone's friend and Anne's partner at work. Terry and Tonya lived next to Susan and Steven. Susan is also close with Melanie and Julie G.

Julie G. is married to Mick and their son Max played ball with Bauer. Down the street from us and Melissa and Chad are Rita and Dr. John. They have three boys—Brandon, Dylan, and Tristan. Brandon is the same age as the girls and has been close with them and Bryce-Terrie and Jason's son since kindergarten too. Dylan and Bauer are the same age and are together *all* the time! Rita runs with Tonya, Rae Ann, and Kelli. Rae Ann is best friends with Paula, who is married to Levi and is an amazing artist. Their daughter is Ellis and is also buddies with Malory, Jordan, Raegan, and Abby. Kelli is married to Matt, but she used to be married to Keith and they have three kids—Kristen, Kory, and Karsen. Kristen was on cheer when my girls were on pom and Karsen is Bauer's age too. He and Dylan are best friends. Tonya is married to Dave and they have two boys—Taylor and Braden. Rae Ann is married to Alan and they live down from Paula and Ronda. Ronda is married to Craig and they have three boys. Craig is the town fireman and Ronda teaches at Grove. Terry and Joey moved to Tulsa but Joey is from here. They have two girls—Maddie and Kennedy. Holly and Terry were friends at OSU, but Holly moved back to Shawnee after college. She has a son named Taylor and also used to live down the street from Rae Ann and Paula. Rae Ann also went to OSU, as did John and April Stobbe. John is our dentist and April is on the school board. They have three kids—Johnny, Emily, and Olivia. Olivia is Bauer's age. Johnny is Creed and Jack's age and Emily is Gage's age, who also dates Matt, Gage's best friend. John's brother is Scott, who has been best friends with Jeff since high school. Scott was married to Renée and they had three girls—Sydney, Taylor, and Scottie. They divorced and Renée married Jeff P. and had Jamen. Jamen and Bauer have always been best buddies. Jeff P. was best friends growing up with

Darrin. Darrin is Chad's other brother and is married to Kristy. They have two boys—Drayden and Jace.

I graduated with Darrin also and Kristi and I were in the same sorority in college. Renée was also in high school with Michael, Jeff, Carol, Terrie, Jason and Russ and Larry. Michael was always roommates with Russ and Larry before they were all married.

Michael is part of a flag football team called old school he's played with for years. Jeff, Chad, and Jeff B. also play. Jeff B. is married to Sarah, and they have three kids—including Creed who is Bauer's age—and Jeff B. coaches their basketball team with Michael as well. Sarah went to high school with all of us too. Russ married Sarah and they have four babies—Wyatt, Ashlin, KK, and Owen. Larry married Kena and they have three babies—Brenner, Cooper, and Addie. Russ and Larry and Michael were all really good coaches together. They coached ball and wrestling with Jeff C. for years. Jeff C. also went to high school with them and married Kathy, who also graduated with Michael and Renee, and they have four kids together too—Taylor, who is my twins' age; Colby, Riley, and Cade, who is Bauer's age. Kathy danced in high school with Nicki, who is also close with April, John's wife. Nicki was Melissa's age in school and also decided to raise her family in Shawnee. She is married to Chris and they have four daughters—Emma, Abby, Harper, and Maggie. Emma and the girls have grown up together and Maggie and Bauer have the same birthday. Nicki is the nurse practitioner at the clinic and when Greg and Jennifer moved to OKC, the girls and I started going to see her. Nicki is best friends with Heidi, Michelle, and Melanie. Michelle is a teacher and she is married to Steve, who is our banker. Melanie is married to John and they have two boys. Heidi is married to Mike and they have three kids too. Their oldest is Erin and she is on the pom squad with Jordan and Raegan and so is Morgan, Steve and Michelle's daughter. Heidi and Michelle are the newest Cheer and Pom moms. For the last few years, pom and cheer moms have been Nicki, Nancy, Jennifer, Sulyne, and Christie, Jessica B., and Kim-Kim's husband, Mike, is also a doctor with John and Tony.

I also have the most amazing dance moms—Christie, Jeree, Courtney, Shai, Su, and Jennifer. Darian, Makynna, and Chandler are also on the pom squad and are very close with Jordan and Raegan. Brooklyn, Makynna, and Jalen are awesome dancers and kids. Anoisty, Jaxie, and Brooke, our Thunder girl, are the teachers but we love them too!

Anoisty owns Dreamcatchers, and we have become like family. Shai is also my neighbor, and her husband is Clark and their daughters are Brooklyn, who dances with us, and Kaitlyn. Kaitlyn is Bauer's age and Brooklyn is Creed and Jack's age. My baseball moms were Summer—of course, she's Langston's mom—Amber, Kristy, Paige and Steph, plus my new baseball mom's-Tanya, Micah, Tracy, Lisa, Missy.

Raegan's boyfriend is Chris. He is best friends with Bryce, Luke, Josh, Bryce, JJ, Dace, Brandon, and Tanner. Chris's mom is Shannon. Shannon is married to Kurt and they also have Jesse and Colton. Jesse has been friends with Chandler for years. Teresa and David have Tiffany and she played soccer with the girls. Teresa is best friends with Amanda who is also Chad's sister. I met Dovie and Debi in Junior Service League and their families own Billy Boy and Paul's Place, two amazing restaurants in town where everyone loves to eat. Dovie lives next door to my mom in the house Melissa and Chad used to live in.

Another one of Bauer's buddies is Seth. Seth's parents are Melanie and Jim. Jim and Michael have also been friends since middle school. Jim used to be married to Pam and they have two boys—Colin and Grant. Pam is remarried to Mike and they also have two kids—Kendall and Aaron. Trevor is Jim's brother and he is married to Holly. She also went to high school with Jim. Pam is close with Kelli Ann and Taryn. Kelli Ann's mom is Karen who is also best friends with Billy and Suzanne who are also close with Russ and Sarah. Taryn is married to Justin, whom I was also close to in high school. They are in League as well with Jessica. Her mom is Cynthia who went to high school with Phyllis. They are close with Lori and Paula, who were the first people I ever met in Shawnee. Down the other side of the neighborhood is Kathy and Charlie. They have Luke and Kara. Luke is best friends with Bryce and Chris and Brandon and all the girls as well. Kathy and I became friends because of kids, but she has been a wonderful friend to me and the girls. Kio and April have five kids. Two of them are boys—Caleb and Christian. Christian dates Sydney, Renee and Scott's daughter, and Caleb played ball with Bauer for years. Kio helped Michael coach and is good friends with Larry. Zane is another friend of all the boys who played ball with Michael and Bauer for years. Bauer loves Zane. His mom is Ryan, whose parents are Barbra and Brian. Brian is somehow related to Chad also. Heck, at this point, we all are!

Although my girls went to Grove, we moved Bauer to South Rock Creek School. It's another great school just like Grove. Josh and Amber's son, Krew, goes there and he played ball with Bauer, too. Also at SRC is Tanner-Dennette and JT's son.

Josh went to Shawnee High School also and coaches all the boys too. JT and Dennette, we met through ball, but now we get to see all of them at Bauer's new school.

Jeff and RaeAnn have three kids—Blakely, Jeffrey, and Jaden. Jeff coached at Shawnee for years, and RaeAnn and I were pregnant at the same time with Jeffrey and my twins. Jaden goes to school with Wyatt and Bauer, and Blakely married Nick—Alex's brother and Jessica's son.

We love these people. We spend weekends and holidays together. Football games and dance competitions. We eat lunch at Benedict St. together on certain days. We've been through weddings and divorces. Births and deaths. We've raised our children together. We cried together when Anne died. We held each other when Tonya's son Taylor died.

Debt, addiction, car wrecks, and cancer.

Success, hope, love, and healing.

I love these people. I'd trust them with my life. Which is a good thing, because I didn't know I'd have to.

Under Water

Do not be afraid, for I have ransomed you.
I have called you by name; you are mine.
When you go through deep waters I will be with you.

—Isaiah 43:1–2 (NLT)

January 2013

I woke up this morning with the same reoccurring dream I'd been having for months. I was underwater. I was drowning. I struggled to reach for the top where the light was shining through. No matter what I did, I never could reach the top of the water. Right when I was about to give up and drown, I'd wake up. I was at a point where I feared waking up. Sweating and in a panic, I'd sit up to catch my breath feeling the water as an enemy. Yet so was the light of day. Yes…I know. Anyone who's had a psychology class can tell you what this means. But I didn't care. To be honest, I didn't have time to deal with it. My alarm goes off as I'm lying in bed staring at the thick dust on my nightstand. If I moved my Bible and all the "feel better" books I don't have time to read, there'd be a perfect dust square. I get the kids up and barely have time to get my hair washed, much less eat. We'd all made it through Christmas. January was the busiest month of the year for our business and the kids' activities were back in full force. Jordan and Raegan were sophomores and Bauer was in the fourth grade. As soon as football was over, we'd go right into basketball. Of course, baseball was pretty much all year round. Jordan and Raegan danced all year traveling to competitions and played soccer for the high school. My children's lives were wonderful. Other than your typical "kid stuff," they were very happy and having a *great* year. I, on the other hand, was a mess. In the midst of every day life—all the lists, all the work, all the errands, all the carpools, all the activities—you forget to put yourself on the list. You forget to put your spouse on the list. We don't pay attention to what we need. You lay your head on the pillow at night and you play the entire next day in your head. If everyone has clean clothes, lunches, and finished homework in their bags, you feel accomplished. We work all day from town to town and by the end of the night we'd all end up at home together with someone asking "Where's my uniform?" or "What's for dinner?" Michael and I could talk on the phone while driving during the day, but once we were home we were lucky if we passed each other in the hallway or on the street driving.

It had been a very long time since that little girl danced to *Grease* in the living room. I had gotten to a place in my life where I didn't even remember who she was. I did enjoy driving all day. I loved to drive. It was kind of like dancing in the living room. I could get in the car, roll down the windows, and just go. I'd turn up the music and come up with all kinds of things to write about. I'd not answer my phone or talk to anyone so I could have some time to myself.

Driving was one of the very few things I had control over. Rolling down those windows and just taking off was very freeing for me. I love it. At this point, trying to be 100 percent to my job and my family was starting to take a toll. I'd make my lists and pay the bills and do my orders for work but the stressing *never* stopped. I'm not sure if worrying and stressing is genetic or environmental or maybe both, but mine was *bad*. Something else I stressed about was the fact that I *smoked*. Yes, me, the little girl with asthma. My asthma had been under control for years and when I was in college I started smoking. I was a theatre major and that's what we did. We were artsy, cool drama people who smoked cigarettes and compared playwrights.

I know it sounds crazy, but I loved to smoke. Growing up, my parents smoked and all my friends did. All the movies with Bette Davis and Robert De Niro, everyone was smoking. Years later, when you realize it stinks and it will kill you, then it's too hard to quit! I did quit off and on and I never smoked while I was pregnant, but like I said before, I really enjoyed it. Of course, my husband hated it! It drove him crazy. He hated the smell, but mostly he was worried about my health. The last few months my health was deteriorating. I didn't really know it at the time. I was never eating and always smoking. It got to be the only thing I looked forward to doing. Don't get me wrong. No one loves their husband and kids more than I do, but I was lost. I knew I wasn't the only one that felt this way, but the guilt makes you not want to admit it. It's scary to look up one day and feel like you're drowning. You're running like crazy and accomplishing nothing. I wanted my voice to be heard, but I didn't have any idea what to say. I used to think about movies and theatre and now I was worried about toilet paper and if we had trash bags. I'm not feeling sorry for myself. I was just sad and feeling like I didn't have a purpose anymore. I felt defeated. Maybe it was a midlife crisis, but it was very real. Michael and I were becoming very distant so it just made it more okay in my mind to smoke. Marriage is hard. You go through all years and the different ages of your kids and you're working so hard and you look up and think, *Do I even like the person who's lying next to me?* At this point, I was so frustrated and tired I thought I'd just deal with it later. I was sad about my self loathing. I used to be positive and hopeful I was the one who told all my friends to find their purpose. I believe there's a reason for who they are and that they can make a difference. Find your dreams and go after them! I had such faith in God and even if it wasn't the path you had intended, the dreams were instilled inside of you for a reason. Everyone was important and all had a purpose. I wasn't sure if I believed that anymore. I didn't want my family to know. I didn't want them to think I didn't love them or I was unhappy with my life. What was bothering me didn't really have anything to do with them. I knew it was my issue. It was something inside of myself, and I was going to try to handle it.

January was a new year. It was a chance for a new attitude and a new motivation for life. That Sunday morning, I walked into church. Brother Todd was a very knowledgeable and motivating minister. Every year he started with a new theme. Up on the stage were two signs and a big photo above the choir seats. The photo was a tiny boat. On the left side was a huge wave about to drown the boat. The two signs on either side said "Getting through the storms of life." I almost fell down. It was as if Brother Todd knew. But he didn't. I'd never told anyone. I thought to myself, *Okay, God is speaking to me.* I had hoped this would be an amazing year. If God was talking to me I was going to listen. I mean, what better theme than how to get through a storm for someone who is drowning.

Forgotten

When you pass through the waters, I will be with you; and
through the rivers, they shall not overwhelm you; when you walk
through fire you shall not be burned, and the flame shall not
consume you.

—Isaiah 43:2 ESV

I will never fail you nor forsake you.

—Hebrews 13:5 ESV

My backyard patio had always been one of my favorite places. I know
it sounds silly, but sitting back there surrounded by all of my flowers
made me smile. It made me feel safe. It gave me peace. Michael and I
have laughed and eaten with our friends and family out there. Bauer
plays ball and the girls practice dance routines. It has always been
where we'd light a fire and hang out with our friends.

My girlfriends and I would call it "roundtable" or "patio night." If
we really needed to catch up if we hadn't seen each other in a while,
we'd call it "Emergency Roundtable" or "Last-minute patio night."
We'd make sure our husbands were fed and the kids were happy and
then we'd all meet. Sometimes it was only an hour, sometimes two or
three, but it helped us get through the week. Just even an hour with
"the girls" can get you through a week of crap.

May 2013

So far, 2013 had not been what I'd hoped. I went into January
knowing it was going to be a great year. I made a list in my head of
how to change my life to make it better. I was going to try to spend

more time with my husband and kids. Not just crazy-rushing-in-the-car time, but real quality time. I was going to work harder and clean my house more, make sure the laundry was always done. I was going to quit smoking again and exercise every day early in the morning. I was going to be happy and appreciate what I had instead of worrying all the time. I really wanted to be happy. I decided to be happy all the time, not just all those funny, crazy moments. I was going to trust God's path for me and quit feeling sorry for myself. Yeah…well… all that went right out the window when my car was broken into. I tried to stay positive but it was hard. They stole my work bag, my purse, and both of my girls' dance bags. Do you know how expensive all those dance shoes are? Oh, it didn't stop there either. The next few months were full of trials and even more "craziness!" All of this new attitude I had turned into a flood in our master bedroom, a small fire in our guest bathroom, multiple deadly tornadoes throughout our state, stress after stress with job, other drama. My reoccurring dream just became worse and more real. I couldn't sleep at night and I hated waking up in the morning. My peaceful patio just became a place where I could go to sneak outside and smoke.

All of those major catastrophes happening one right after the other was unbearable. I had listened to Brother Todd's sermons about praying and fighting but it wasn't working. I kept wondering what I was doing wrong. I would drive down the road thinking about that girl. That girl who was full of hope and love and purpose. I thought I was different. The girl who was going to do something that mattered. I had a plan for my life. I felt so defeated. How was I supposed to make a difference in my own life? How was I supposed to conquer the world when I could barely conquer a shower? Everyone else seemed to be doing it. Why couldn't I?

So I just kept driving and working and trying to stay away from the tornadoes. My twins' sixteenth birthday was steadily approaching. No matter what stress and chaos was going on, I was going to make this super special. I had called a few of the girls' friends and they were helping me plan a surprise party for them. The party was planned for the weekend after their actual birthday. They would think we weren't doing anything for them and BAM! They'd be surprised. It was a big deal for them and we wanted to make it as special as possible.

The week prior to their birthday I had received a call from April C.. I hadn't seen April in years, but we all know we love each other and can always pick up where we'd left off. A few weeks ago, our sweet friend Samantha had lost her child. Sweet Rex died in his crib from SIDS. The sadness and the heartbreak is indescribable. April called to let me know she was flying Samantha in to have some "friend" time and wanted all of us to get together. I almost cried and told her I'd get a hold of everyone and make sure we were all here together. Not only would it do Samantha good to be with girls who had loved her and known her her entire life, but I needed them too. Thinking about what Sam has been going through reminded me what really matters— loving our people. So I called Brooke, Danielle, Angie, and Melisa and we were all set to be together. Brooke was coming from Kansas City, Danielle was coming from Spiro, Sam from San Antonio, April from Norman, and Angie and I lived here. They were all coming. Melisa was meeting us too and we were set. Work, surprise party, pom camp, baseball...it was already a crazy June and the only thing that helped lessen my stress was to smoke. If I was worried about Samantha, I'd smoke. If I was worried about my quota at work, I'd smoke. If I was fighting with Michael, I'd smoke. Whatever it was, I'd smoke. Trying to give everything to everyone and do it perfectly was starting to take a toll on me. It was impossible. I started to become angry.

June 11, 2013

I started this day praying. As spiritual as I was, I wasn't in a great place. I woke up in my bedroom and would step over the mildewed carpet. We'd been so busy we had not found the time to have it replaced yet. I was getting ready to spend the day with my girls. Today was their sixteenth birthday. I didn't feel right today. I was wheezing but of course I was still smoking. I just felt angry. I know you're not supposed to say this but I was really angry at *God*. I was angry my aunt died and I didn't talk to her. I was angry Samantha's baby died. I was angry that Erin and Alex's mom Anne had died. She was my *friend*. It had been years but I'd never really dealt with it. I was angry that I had tried so hard to have a good year and all these awful setbacks kept happening to us. I was angry that I felt like my husband didn't love me. I was angry I didn't get to spend enough time with my kids. I had prayed and prayed and nothing was happening. I had done everything I was supposed to do and he had not answered *one* prayer. I was angry Tonya's son Taylor died. I was angry people I loved were hurting. I was angry God had given me dreams that would never be fulfilled. I was angry I would write and write and no one wanted it. I didn't know what to do with all this anger. I had to put it away, It was Jordan and Raegan's birthday.

I didn't travel. I picked up Bauer after school and he and Michael left for baseball. The girls hung out with friends since they "thought" we didn't have anything special planned. I stood on my patio, in deep thought. It had been a long day and an even longer night. Everything about my life started to flood my head. I looked up to the sky and the moon was shining so bright it lit up the entire yard. So many stars sparkled over the sky, I felt so small. I smoke one cigarette after another. I'd never felt like a failure before. I truly was drowning, just like my dream. I was angry that God had forgotten about me. I used to see happiness and hope and color in everything I looked at. Now I was colorless. Lifeless. Full of resentment and anger. Full of turmoil. Not a speck of peace or joy except when I looked at my children, but then I of course had guilt. Guilt that I wasn't good enough and that I didn't just fail myself but I had failed Michael, the girls, Bauer, my parents, anyone I'd ever lectured to about "following your *dreams*," I thought it would have been better if I just gave up. So I did. I looked up at the dark sky and the bright moon, threw my hands up, and said, "Okay. I'm done. God, you forgot about me so I give up. I've done everything wrong. I'm done."

I went in.

I went to bed.

I fell asleep and

I died.

Into the Calm

He made the storm be still, and thus the waves of the sea were hushes.

—Psalm 107:29 (ESV)

Therefore you also must be ready; for the son of man is coming at an hour you do not expect.

—Matthew 24:44 (ESV)

Sometimes parents need to give their children a timeout. I wasn't ready for what happened next...

This was the moment everything stopped. Everything *went away*. It was dark. It wasn't cold or hot. It felt like I was flying. Flying like a beautiful bird floating in the sky. The wind was going through my hair, my skin, and my heart. Joy filled my soul and I realized I was floating on a very soft, fluffy carpet—like a magic carpet. I wasn't scared. I wasn't afraid of the height. I didn't doubt why I was there. The darkness faded and it was so beautiful. It was as if a huge stage curtain opened and there were beautiful colors and clouds. There was water everywhere. Crisp, beautiful, clean, warm waterfalls everywhere you looked. The light was brilliant as the water fell into the clouds. The white pureness of the clouds was soft to the touch of my skin.

I turned to my left and he was sitting next to me. I knew who he was. I had never known such peace. I had never felt so safe. Huge pictures of my life started flashing before me like a slide show. He never said anything. We just watched the pictures of my life together.

- Sitting at a small table and my dad (looking quite young) playing peek-a-boo with me as a baby.

- My mom curling my hair in our bathroom. I was about five and very tired of standing there and she was saying, "Beauty is painful."

- Christmas with my brother, Pat, and sister, Allyson, and my grandma Stewart. My cousins and aunt Judy opening gifts.

- Riding in the truck next to my grandpa headed to the coffee shop in Stroud, OK.

- Canyon Church Camp, playing in the neighborhood, riding bikes with my friends, high school graduation, driving around in my Grand Am with the windows down with Angie and Brooke.

- college sorority bid day pictures, working on movie sets.

- Jordan and Raegan dancing in their Disney high heels and sunglasses as two year olds.

- Thanksgiving. My mother's table set with place cards and orange leaves. Her noodles and dressing and the sound of football in the background.

- Going to a Tesla concert with Melisa and Chad, Pam, Michael, Kim, Chad S., Wade, Mandy, and Russ. Kissing Michael for the first time on the way home.

- Michael and me in Santa Fe watching the OU–Texas game on our way to get married.

- Michael talking to me when they first pulled Bauer out of my belly in the operating room.

- Bauer on the floor with the girls when he crawled for the first time and they were cheering.

- Bauer, Jordan, and Raegan all asleep on the living room floor and the TV still on.

- Eating sushi with Anne, Tonya, Terry, and Holly.

- Patio night with Summer and all the girls.

- Halloween party with our friends and the town band. My Dad Rocks.
- Watching Jordan and Raegan dance.
- Watching Bauer pitch.
- Watching Michael coach Bauer.
- Walking in the neighborhood with Melisa and Terrie, laughing.
- Lunch at Benedict Street with the girls.

All of these joyous moments in my life flashing before my eyes and tears of pure happiness rolling down my face. At that moment, Jesus turned to me and said, "See, you haven't done everything wrong."

All of a sudden, we start to pass by the most beautiful *wall*. Outside standing against the wall was a line of people waving at me as I went by. The feeling of "breath taken away" is an understatement for what I was feeling. I stood up and started waving and yelling like crazy! "Hey. Oh my gosh, I love you! I miss you!"

Against this beautiful white-and-gold brick wall, standing in clouds, smiling and waving at me were all the people I had dearly loved and lost in my life.

My grandpa stood waving with his John Wayne hat and my grandma Presley on his arm. My beautiful friend Anne stood smiling and waving. She had on shorts and her marathon number pinned to her shirt.

My sweet Grandma Stewart had her big rings and her "old lady" loafers and skirt on. Her hair curled as if she'd just been to the beauty shop.

My aunt Judy. It was tough to see her. When she died we were not on the best of terms. It was an incredible feeling. All the pain or anger I'd felt was gone. She was smiling and waving.

I waved and waved and jumped up and down. Hoping to make sure they all saw me! I remember saying, "I thought Anne would be with her own family."

He said, "She is."

Then I crashed—crashed deep into water. As I was floating back up to the top, I was at peace. I wasn't kicking and panicking like in my dreams.

I floated peacefully to the top. Through the light beams, a big, strong hand came through the water to help me up into the canoe. I was refreshed. I felt renewed. He was sitting in one canoe and I was in the other. The water was so calm and beautiful. It was like glass. Birds were chirping. The trees were slightly blowing in the gentle breeze. The colors of everything were so rich and vibrant. I had seen trees and waterfalls before, but nothing as pure as these. It was as if I was seeing everything for the first time. I had no idea why or where I was. I never once doubted or questioned it. I was just at peace and overwhelmed with emotion. I turned to Jesus and I said, "You didn't forget about me."

"Of course not," he said, "I've been here every step."

Sitting in the canoe talking with Him, I can't describe the power of emotions. I wanted to fall to my knees and pray thanks for his scars. I wanted to ask him so many questions about life and why things happen the way they do. But I didn't. I sat in a trance. I had never felt so safe in my life. Words would have just clouded the space I was in with *him*.

I said to him , "I want to stay here." Tears flowed and my body felt very heavy. A warm joy and feeling of security surged through my soul and nothing could hurt me. I felt no pain. No fear, no sadness, *no worry*. In fact, I didn't know what "worry" or "anger" meant. I lay there, relaxed, in the canoe with the soft warmth of the sun on my face, and I heard his voice say, "Your life has purpose, Julie."

I said, "I really could stay here."

He continued, "It won't be easy on you. You will find it again. You can't just believe. You have to have faith."

I didn't really know the depth of what he was saying. Those are very simple, yet massive statements. I listened to every word as if in a deep sleep but I didn't really know what it meant. Not, of course, until later. I just lay there soaking in the words just like the warm sun. It felt like I would lay there forever next to him. I feel strange trying to explain it. Like trying to explain loving your child. *Impossible.* I fell into a deep sleep. Very slowly. I kept hearing "can't do it alone" and "it's all right in front of you there" and "great purpose," "great journey."

I sat up and said, "No, I want to stay here." I needed more time to take it all in. The breeze and his voice and the colors. The sounds. The feeling.

Jesus shook his head and said, "It's not time."

I thought that meant I could stay. All of a sudden, I started soaring. It felt amazing. I was *so* happy. Going through the clouds, I felt like I was flying again. It's hard to think about the joy and hope I was feeling. It's hard to wrap my brain around what happened up there. At the very moment I felt renewed and reborn, somewhere below me, I was dying. My family was suffering. The last thing I remember him saying to me was "Don't forget to take me with you next time."

I said, "What?"

He replied, "You're not finished yet."

I said, "I don't wanna fight anymore."

I heard, "I'm fighting for you," as everything started to fade.

I wasn't where I'd call "heaven." Maybe outside heaven in the front yard. I saw the gates and Jesus was with me but it felt like a joyride. A time out with Jesus. I didn't know until later, what it really meant…

Waking Up in New Mexico

He reached down from heaven
and took hold of me;
He pulled me out of deep waters.
He rescued me from my powerful enemy
and from those who hated me,
for they were too strong for me.
They confronted me in the day of my distress,
but the Lord was my support.
He brought me out to a spacious place;
He rescued me because He delighted in me.

—Psalm 18: 16-19 (HCSB)

The water felt like a cleanse. Thought and situations were in the back of my mind. At this point in my life, being alive for me meant that it was "always something."

Something to worry about.

Something to stress about.

Something to be upset about.

Something to...but now, this floating and being free was magical.

Dipping into this water and feeling this cleansed gave me a warmth and yet a coolness I'd never felt. When I was under water, it occurred to me this was like the nightmare I'd had for years. Except this was Heaven. My thoughts and fears had *shifted* and it was no longer a nightmare. It was truly a dream. About that time...

I opened my eyes, and I was in New Mexico. I was in a bar, which was funny because I'd just been with Jesus and I dropped into this bar in Red River, New Mexico.

I'd been here *before*. Then again, maybe I hadn't.

There was a pool table with a dog.

The lights were dim.

I'm not sure how long I soared dancing and floating, but the next thing I remembered, I was in this place I'd seen before. The place was empty except for me, my husband, Michael, a guy I didn't know wiping down the bar, and a dog. The dog was asleep on the pool table and the only face I could see was Michael's. No one was allowed to buy a drink unless they bought the dog a shot first.

The state of New Mexico and I have a kind of funny history. I've traveled to and through there many times in my life. Michael and I stopped in Santa Fe on our way to get married. We had walked through the "miraculous staircase" church and watched the OU–Texas football game in a restaurant there right in the middle of the downtown square area. Before Bauer was even born, we spent a week in Red River with all of our friends and years later went one Christmas with all the kids and Chad and Melisa to Angelfire. New Mexico is a safe, happy place for me. I think of the joy and love and anticipation of marrying Michael. The cold air and football on in the background. The church was so beautiful and calming. Some of our best family and friend moments were spent in New Mexico. It's the state I was in when I found out my friend Anne had died. It's also the state Melisa was in when she found out I had died.

I was very sleepy, but I could hear their voices talking about skiing in New Mexico. All of a sudden, the room I was in started to fade and I felt very weighed down. Now I had no idea where I was. My chest and head felt so big and heavy that I couldn't move. Like a three hundred-pound block had crashed into my chest. The only part of my entire body I could move were my eyes, but everything was dark. I remember the two male voices and a beeping sound. My breathing was very, very sharp and slow. For some reason, I couldn't talk. I started to open my eyes and I heard Michael's voice at my ear. He said, "Please don't fight. Stay calm. If you fight you'll die. Please don't fight, just breathe."

I'm thinking, *What in the world is he talking about? Fighting?* Why would I fight He obviously had no idea where'd I been. You see, peace and calm were emotions I'd always wanted to feel. I never realized it was a place. A real place, and I had been there. I tried to tell him, but

I couldn't talk. Where was I? I thought I was in New Mexico. Who was this other voice I could hear? I lifted my right hand as if asking to write. I had no idea why I couldn't move. Or why I couldn't talk. I had no idea where I was or why I was there. I just remember not being afraid. I knew where I'd been. I somehow relayed to Michael to tell a story to the guy in the room about one of our New Mexico trips. Michael was so happy I was awake he said to the nurse, "She wants me to tell you this story about the dog in a bar, asleep on the pool table. As he proceeded to tell the story, the man was shocked. He asked Michael, "How long ago was that?"

Michael said, "Maybe nine or ten years ago?"

Apparently we were *not* in a bar. We were in a hospital room. The guy talking was a nurse.

He said, "Wow. Okay. That's a really good sign."

I was thinking, *Sign? Sign of what? What in the world happened?*

My chest was so heavy and flat, but once again I didn't feel pain. I remember my children crying and smiling. I remember hugging Michael's face with my right hand. The joy I felt seeing my kids and Michael is unexplainable. It felt like a broken heart mending and a warm feeling of healing surrounded me. I remember crying a lot, but I had to do it very slowly because for some reason I couldn't talk or breathe. My mom and dad and brother were there. My brother was joking about my dad being nervous and fidgety in the room and knocking things over. I thought, *Okay, how long have I been in here?* My mom was just smiling and crying. Now that I think back, so many family and friends came to see me that morning. The nurse showed me a picture in a frame and asked if I knew the picture. Did I know where I was? The picture was taken at New Mexico Angelfire when we were skiing. It was in a frame that said, "It had to be you," which is one of my favorite songs from my favorite movie *When Harry Met Sally*. My first thought was, *I didn't buy that frame, Oh my, how long have I been here? And why is she asking me if I know the picture? Why wouldn't I?*

Michael said, "*You had an asthma attack, and you got really sick.*" I wanted so badly to talk. His eyes got really big and said, "No, no, don't mess with the vent. You can't get another one."

What? An asthma attach? Uhm...okay. But I still wondered why I couldn't talk or move.

I was so confused. Somehow I asked, "What day is it? Did I miss the girls' birthday? Did I miss Father's Day?" I was so upset. My dad was crying. Mike and Debi were in there too. All of my family and friends. Everyone kept coming in and out, crying.

Michael said, "It's okay. You didn't miss the girls' birthday. Do you remember eating with them?"

I shook my head no. Honestly I didn't remember much of anything. I knew who everyone was but just nothing else yet. I somehow relayed to them I wanted Michael to go to the country club and get my dad and his dad a shirt from the clubhouse for Father's Day. They kind of laughed and said, "No, no, it's okay. You're awake. That's all we care about." Bauer hugged me, and the girls just kept smiling at me, grabbing and hugging my legs. I was so confused. Greg had brought me a clipboard so I could try to communicate with everyone.

The room was dark and quiet. There was a constant beep...beep... beep...from the machines, but other than that the feeling was very still. ICU stands for Intensive Care Unit. All the patients on this floor are very, very sick. Most of the patients are older, so when this floor of nurses and doctors met my crazy family and friends, well, let's just say it was a shock and very entertaining. The one thing no one has ever accused me or my family of is being quiet.

Doctors and nurses kept coming in and checking on me. My girls and my mom and Melisa just kept smiling but *no one* would tell me *anything!*

Dr. Greg Blair, his wife Jennifer, Catherine, and the twins, Erin and Allie, came in to see me. He was trying to very carefully ask me how I was and making very lightly the reason I was there. He kept looking at Michael and I could tell they weren't telling me everything. Was Greg here as a doctor, or as a friend? Where was I?

When Jenn told me that the twins had been there the entire time, it hit me what Jesus had ment. He said, "Anne was with her 'own.' And her 'own' was with mine. They had all been with me the entire time.

Jenn was crying, and said, "You're beautiful."

I thought, *Well, I know that's not true.*

My friend Summer kept poking her head in and smiling and Summer always made me laugh. She would come in and poke her head through the ICU curtian and say, "This is no way to get me out of bed before 10AM! If you wanted me to drive to OKC, you could have just said so." She hated to drive and I was the one that always drove us all over the state to all of the ball games. I also joked with her about being lazy, so now she could thrown it back in my face since now I was the one that couldn't get out of bed. Even in ICU, she was still making me laugh. Even still, I didn't know what was going on.

Kelli came in to see me. She was crying and said, "Don't ever do that to us again!"

I hadn't seen Kelli in a while. I wondered why she was so upset.

I looked at her very confused and thought, *What did I do?* I could see Michael next to me waving, as if saying "No, no." Nicki came in and she said nothing, which wasn't like her, except "You are a beautiful miracle." I knew something was wrong. Okay, not sure what everyone was trying to protect me from but it was sweet. I wanted so badly to tell everyone where I had been, but I couldn't talk, and as good and happy as I felt, I was sorry for my family's sadness. As happy as the faces were, I could see there had been a lot of pain and anguish.

Everything and everyone looked crooked to me. About every few minutes, my family and Michael would check a bag next to my bed. Everyone was always quietly talking around me but when they'd look at me, they'd just say "You look so beautiful," "You're doing so great, Mom." People had to leave my room for hours at a time so they could hook me up to machines. I had no idea what was happening but I just kept praying, "God, Jesus, are you still there?" Was it all a dream? It couldn't have been. It was so real. I know it was real. As much as I knew I loved my family, what I needed to know now was what happened to me while I was up there. I needed to know why I couldn't move or breathe. How did an asthma attack turn into this? How long had I been here? I needed to know why Michael had told everyone not to tell me anything and not to upset me. I needed to know why the greatest experience of my life was my family's *worst*.

Finding Out What Happened

He leads me beside the still waters.
He restores my soul;
He leads me in the paths of righteousness
For His name's sake.
Yea, though I walk through the valley of the shadow of death,
I will fear no evil;
For You are with me

—Psalm 23:2–4 (NKJV)

Finding out what really happened didn't come easily. No one wanted me to know. I think I was dealing with so much physically after I woke up they felt like I just needed to focus on my breathing. Even after everything I was dealing with while I was awake, I still needed to know what happened that brought me to the moment I was now in. Lying in bed on a ventilator and not being able to move wasn't easy. Different friends and family took shifts to stay with me through the night. That way Michael could get some rest. He didn't sleep or change his clothes at all the weeks I was "asleep," and he was doing pretty rough. I remember Melisa and Jordan in the ICU room in the middle of the night, and every time I'd look over at them they'd drop their heads and act like they were asleep. I was so *irritated*! I'd think, *Why? Why are they doing that? Why don't they want me trying to talk?*

I heard people say "coding" and "many times" and I didn't know what that meant. I did not understand why no one wanted me to know what exactly brought me to this day. Nicki would pat me on the arm and say, "That's for a different day." My mom just cried and held my hand. My friends just smiled creepy joker smiles the entire time they'd talk to me and all my girls did was write in journals—tell me

I was beautiful—and say, "Bauer, tell Mom you love her. Tell Mom she's beautiful."

I knew Bauer loved me more than anyone but he seemed tired and uncomfortable. My dad couldn't come in without knocking stuff down and hitting and pulling all my cords. He was so funny. Michael's parents and family never left, my family never left, my friends never left. Michael was so strong but way too protective. I knew something was up.

I knew my left hand, for some reason, wouldn't move. My right arm and hand worked fine. I had notebooks to write on and tried hard to communicate. My words were not going on to the paper the same way they were coming out of my head. Everyone had a very hard time making any sense of what I was trying to say and they all seemed afraid of my left hand. In fact, one night I thought I'd make a joke. Near the door was a loud banging sound. It went on and on all through the night. Well, come to find out the sounds was a machine that cleaned and disinfected all the floors of the rooms in the hospital. It ran automatically and it would hit the wall and clean the other side and so on and so on. Well, Chad—Melisa's husband and Michael's best friend—was a complete freak about cleaning. He was OCD at its finest. When we went to New Mexico, he made us wait to go in the house until he had bleached it all. I mean the kitchens, the bathrooms—everything. We love him but we all know he's that way, so funny me, I was gonna make a joke of "Hey you need to get one of those machines for Chad." Haha. Yeah, well, thirty minutes later Melisa and Jordie still had no idea what the heck I was talking about. I was trying to say it without being able to say it. I guess it's hard to make jokes when you can't talk—even Melisa at one point leaned down and said, "Oh, you wanna see Chad?" I pounded my right hand on that clipboard and waved as if to say, "No, no. Never mind." After they took so long to figure out what I was trying to say, it wasn't funny anymore. Forget telling jokes! It was sweet how hard everyone was trying but I was at a point of frustration. I would hear different nurses saying things and knew everyone was keeping the truth from me, assuming I was too fragile. I've been called a lot of things in my life but fragile wasn't one of them. So over a period of weeks, I put the pieces together and figured out what happened to me.

Although I have no memory of that time or many weeks prior, I am able to write about what happened from the stories of everyone involved and my medical records. No one can imagine what it was like to find out what actually happened to me. It's as if everyone is talking about someone else. The pain my family went through is unimaginable. The strength and prayers are humbling. When I found out, I couldn't stop crying. I was in shock but I was truly sad and guilty for what everyone who loved me had been through over the weeks. I now knew why Michael didn't want me to know...

Crashing

Come to me, all you who are weary and burdened, and I will give you rest.

—Matthew 11:28 (NIV)

And he said to them, "Why are you afraid, O you of little faith?"
Then he rose and rebuked the wind and the sea; and there was a great calm.

—Matthew 8:26 ESV

It was June 12, around 4:55 AM. The early morning after, I told God I'd given up and went to bed. The morning after the girls' sixteenth birthday. Raegan's phone started ringing. As she answered in her sleep, she heard my voice say, "Raegan, help me."

You see, that night I had slept upstairs in the playroom. I could still smell the fire from our bathroom downstairs. I was already having breathing problems from everything else—the stress, the smoking. I thought I would breathe and sleep better being upstairs

Raegan ran into the room and I could barely talk. I asked her to take me to the emergency room. She said she went to get her shoes and I started freaking out. The breathing machine wasn't working and I needed help. I wasn't breathing. She said I was panicked and acting crazy. She called 911. Jordan heard Raegan talking, so she got up and went into Raegan's room. She went downstairs to wake her dad and tell him what was going on. He was very calm and talked to the 911 dispatcher. They arrived and rushed upstairs. The EMTs stabilized my breathing. They debated whether or not to take me in but decided to go ahead and do so. Michael followed them to the hospital in our car. He had the girls stay behind because Bauer was still asleep. He and the girls concluded they would probably just take me in, give me another treatment, and we'd both be home in about an hour. Bauer would sleep through the whole thing.

An hour and a half passed and Michael called Raegan. He told her it was a little worse than they had thought and they needed to wake up Bauer and get to the ER. The girls were not prepared for what they were about to go through. They had no idea it would be months before they'd pull back into our driveway.

So many things happened in such a small amount of time. Arriving in the ER in Shawnee, I took a turn for the worse. The doctors and nurses at Shawnee are not only good at their jobs, but they are like family to us. My nurse, Kelli, I had known for years. Our kids had always gone to school together and we spent years in Junior Service League together. My other nurse practitioner was Niki. She and I went to high school together, raised our kids in the same church and schools. Nicki was a pom Mom and who I saw at the hospital clinic when I was sick. Once Dr. Greg Blair had left Shawnee, I always saw Nicki. Dr. Tony was our neighbor across the street for years. I watched his three girls grow into beautiful, young women. Everyone knew everyone there. I either grew up with them, or was their neighbor, friend, baseball mom, or pom mom. Dr. Mike lived down the street next to Dr. John. I was friends with their wives and *loved* their children. I'm sure going into that ER and seeing me on the gurney was not easy for Kelli when she got to work that day. She heard there was a seriously critical patient down the hall. She didn't expect to see Michael step out of the room.

It's hard to describe my behavior at the ER that morning. To say I was violent is probably a good description. They were trying to sedate me and I was fighting. They put a ventilator down my throat and I ripped it out. They put a central line in my groin and I ripped it out. In fact, blood squirted all over Dr. Mike's shirt.

I'm still not clear why this attach was so bad. My lungs and tubes just closed. They stabilized me enough to get me up to the ICU. The attack was so severe, and I was fighting them so violently they had to sedate me to calm me down.

In the ICU, I started to go into code blue. My lungs were failing and my entire body was shutting down. I had so little oxygen getting to my heart and brain. I was hot and I couldn't breathe. The first time I crashed they got me stabilized. Kelli went out to tell my family I was stable but I probably wouldn't make it through another code blue. Dr. Greg, Jennifer, Erin and Alex were already headed to Shawnee. Word spread very quickly through the hospital to the clinic what was happening to me. The doctors and nurses starting coming over to find out what was going on. Nicki was there and was trying to make some sense out of this reality. Nicki was the doctor I saw on a regular basis. Even though she knew I was weazing more frequently, it wasn't bad enough to have caused this. Michael had asked for prayers on Facebook, which is not like him, but he knew I needed them and he was starting to feel helpless and scared. My family and some friends started showing up at the hospital. I coded for a second time.

Coding is when a patient goes into cardiac arrest and, or respiratory failure. I was in both. My heart kept stopping. My family says that sounds of the alarms going off and the "code blue" being said all over the floor still haunts them. Melisa and her family were driving back from New Mexico as fast as they could. She called Jordan and said, "What's going on?"

Jordan, crying, said, "I don't know. 'Code blue' keeps going off and the nurse and doctors keep telling us to prepare for the worst. Dad, mema, and papa [my parents] are in the room with my mom. My dad is bent over with his hands on his knees like he can't breathe and mema and papa are just crying." They all knew if I coded again I wouldn't survive. By this time most of my family and friends had made it to the hospital.

Kelli and the respiratory therapist named Cammie were in the room when I coded again. My heart was just not wanting to keep beating.

This was the third time and it took them fourteen minutes to get my heart back to beating again. Fourteen minutes is a long time to be flatlined. The doctors knew this was not good. Cammie was on top of the table, leaning over me, doing chest compressions, for fourteen minutes. She didn't stop at two or three minutes. She didn't stop at six and let me go, she kept pushing and pushing and fighting for me to live. They all told my family the chances of my making it through the night were very slim. By this time, the waiting room and the hallways were full of my family and friends.

People brought so much food. Baskets of toiletries, games, food, magazines. Flowers and even cupcakes for the nurses and doctors. People by the dozens lined up praying for me and my family. When I coded for the third time and was out fourteen minutes, my body went into DIC. DIC is a serious disorder in which the proteins that control blood clotting become over active. Very few people survive DIC. I had a heart attack and then a stroke. Luckily, my cousin Brent, who is a fireman, used his tools to cut my wedding ring off before my hand exploded

Here I am, thirty-eight years old, and I had an asthma attack that turned into numerous code blues, a heart attack, DIC, a stroke from the lack of oxygen, and kidney failure. DIC caused my left hand to have what is called a hand ischemia. It swelled up so bad it looked like a black softball glove. The medicine they were giving me was supposed to help my blood flow in my heart and lungs so my other organs were compromised. Coding so many times also caused rhabdonyolysis, damage to my skeletal muscles, which also affected my kidneys. My body was holding an enormous amount of fluid because all of my organs had shut down.

One of the doctors came out and said to Michael and everyone in the waiting room, "We might have to amputate the hand."

Michael said, "Which hand is it? As long as it is not the right one."

The doctor said, "No, it's the left one."

Michael said, "Fine, as long as it's not the right hand, she won't care. That's the hand she writes with."

Once again, the staff told my family, my friends, doctors, and nurses, I more than likely would not live through the night. My friends and family started to get upset with the nurses and doctors for saying that. They didn't wanted to hear it anymore. They believed I would live. Then, once again, I coded. They brought me back and stabilized me. Even if I survived, I would probably be in a vegetative state. I only had a 20 percent oxygen level at best and no physical response to anything or anyone. Dr. Tony, Dr. Greg, Dr. Holland, Dr. Mike, and Dr. John were there. My kids and parents and family and friends slept in chairs and on the floor. Now, everyone *was just waiting*. At one point I did respond physically. I was kicking my feet. Although it was just a physical response, or maybe just a reflex, my family believed I was still in there somewhere. Everyone tried to tell them, "I think she is trying to tell you she is hot."

No one left the hospital. Michael would not leave my side. He didn't care that the nurses said there was no hope. He didn't care that even Greg said I probably wouldn't wake up. Michael sat by the bed and played classical music next to my ear and talked to me the entire night. Greg had even talked to his girls on the way to Shawnee about being there for them the same way my girls had been there when their mom, Anne, died. He was trying to prepare everyone My girls would not say good-bye to me. My family refused to as well. All of my friends believed I would live. The entire town stopped what they were doing to pray for me. My pom and dance moms. All the *ball* moms, kids, and coaches. People I'd sat next to for years at church and school, the Junior Service League, my friends from high school were all here because we were supposed to have dinner that weekend. Now they were all eating in a hospital cafeteria Everyone was with me praying for me. Erin and Alex had been through such loss and were there to be a support for what Jordan and Raegan were about to go through. Tracy brought them new bibles for insight and support.

Bauer's friends from school and baseball were there with him. My parents' friends and Michael's parents' friends were all there. People who had known me my whole life and people who had never met me, were there and praying for me. I wasn't going to live. No one wanted the morning to show itself. Thinking about it now, I have no idea how my family made it through the night.Nicki took all of Dr. Holland's patients so he could sit with me that day and nurse Sylvia watched me through the night. Kelli had clocked out so she could stay with me.

The next morning, Michael thought he saw my eyes open. He talked to me and said my name and I looked at him. He told the nurse and she went to get Dr. Tony and Dr. Holland. They believed it was probably just a reflex but it was worth a try. Dr. Tony got right in my face and yelled, "Julie! Julie!"

I opened my eyes and looked right at him. I was responsive. I think it was a huge shock. No one could believe it. The word spread that I was responsive and even more prayers went up.

The main concern now was making sure I was stable enough to transport to Oklahoma City St. Anthony's. Greg was one of the head doctors there and he and his team were ready for me. You see, even though I responded to my name and the voices, the big concern was that my brain and my kidneys would not wake up. On June 14, I was transported to OKC St. Anthony's. They told Michael to go ahead and the ambulance would meet him there. Michael and my brother left for OKC and my kids went to get some blankets and things from my mom's. Everyone had a job to help out, and then head to OKC's Saint Anthony Hospital. Michael's parents were helping him and Jordan and Raegan's friends came to let our dog out before they all headed to the city.

June 14

Michael waited and waited on the ambulance. It wasn't showing up. It was supposed to be right behind him. His heart sank. He thought I had died on the way to Oklahoma City. You can imagine his relief when my ambulance pulled up forty-five minutes later. They got me to the ICU and that's when the real work began. Dr. Greg and his team of doctors were ready for me. The next few weeks were a waiting game.

The main concern now was that my body and brain would not wake up. Even though I was responsive in Shawnee and stable enough to move, they put me in a deep medically induced coma, so my body would quit fighting. My body and brain were asleep. The doctors immediately hooked me up to dialysis, because my kidneys had shut down. My lungs were very tight. All of my bones from the ribs up to my neck were broken. My brain was swelling, and my left hand would probably have to be amputated. They needed to do an echocardiogram to see what the damage was on my heart and an MRI to see what the stroke damage was on my brain.

I had the best doctors in the state. Dr. Baluja was in charge of my kidneys. Dr. McKinnis was in charge of my lungs. Dr. Cheema was in charge of my brain. Dr. Kirk was in charge of my infections. Dr.

Blair was in charge of everything, including my family. His ability to explain medical jargon in laymen's terms was so helpful. It was so hard, especially for my kids, to understand.

My body was confused and decided to sleep. I wasn't making any urine at all and that was why dialysis was so important. Basically it had just become a watch and wait. At this point, it truly was a miracle I was even alive. Every now and then I'd wake up for a bit and then go back into my deep sleep. As the days went on it was a lot of waiting and watching. On June 18, I opened my eyes for a bit. The DIC was improving and they believed my breathing was as well. Dr. McKinnis wanted to see if he took out the vent if I could still breathe on my own. He took it out and I stopped breathing. Because of all the broken bones, my chest was caving in. My sternum was pushing against my heart and I stopped breathing and my heart stopped beating. So he put the vent back in and I was better. I really just needed more time. I also needed to make urine. I hadn't yet. Not even one drop—for a week. It wasn't good. I was continually on dialysis. My muscles started improving but my body weight was still ten liters over. I weighed 160 pounds. I was way overhydrated because my kidneys were not flushing out. All my fluids started leaking into my tissues. I blew up. Basically I looked like the Michelin Man.

June 19

I was still asleep. I had still only released a few drops of urine, but my DIC was almost resolved, which is a miracle in itself. My hand was still really black and swollen but my oxygen levels were improving.

June 20

The doctors put me on new meds for my hand. I was still on the ventilator, and although I still had no sign of urinating yet, my DIC was completely clear. What a miracle!

June 21

Dr. McKinnis still was not able to take the vent out of my throat. My sternum was still broken and not attached to my ribs so he didn't want to risk anything. Although I was still "asleep," my white blood cell count was going up. I had central lines connected to my lungs and heart for the medications and the dialysis.

Days Later

I woke up.

With no memory and as you know, in "New Mexico."

My First Breath

Don't be afraid, for I am with you.
Don't be discouraged, for I am your God.
I will strengthen you and help you.
I will hold you up with my victorious right hand.

—Isaiah 41:10 (NLT)

Waking up, I knew I was done fighting. What I didn't know was that just ahead of me was the fight of my life. Have you ever been in a situation where you are completely helpless? You have no choice but to trust the people who are taking care of you. Even after waking up, my life was never stable. I fought every single day just to live. I was so confused. I felt like God and Jesus had taken me to such a place of peace, and then brought me back to this? Really? I didn't understand. Jesus said it wouldn't be easy but I had no idea what he was talking about. As I lay there, I felt these very painful twinges in my lower back. I kept telling them that something was wrong. I think they thought that my back was probably just sore from lying in this hospital bed for so, so long. The weight gain and my organs shutting down was the source of my pain. I kept telling Greg, "No, no. Something is wrong." I just knew. The doctors sent me in for a CT scan of my back and stomach. What they found was not good. I was internally bleeding from the blood thinners. They gave me the blood thinners for all the blood clots and it had caused some sort of an abscess in my lower back.

This scan was actually the very first test I remember having. While I was asleep, they took many CTs, MRIs, and x-rays, but now being awake and wheeled downstairs and moved to a table, I was scared. Not to mention the fact that I was still on the ventilator. As I'm lying on the table, I heard a sweet voice whisper in my ear, "Hi, Julie. It's

Taylor. Taylor Haddad. You're so brave. You're doing great." Tears just started flowing down my face. I felt like God had sent her right in that moment. I needed someone and *no one else* I knew could be in that room. Taylor was Dr. Tony's daughter. She was a student and was just observing at this hospital the day I happened to be in there for tests. It was a humiliating situation. They put me on my stomach and I just remember thinking, *Thanks goodness I'd been tanning.*

I went back to the ICU and Dr. McKinnis came in and was considering taking my vent out. As still as I had to lay, I felt my entire body do flip flops. I wanted out so badly. For me not being able to talk was difficult. I really don't know what I would have done without my nurses. I remember always looking at my nurses with tears and thinking I'll never forget what they've done for me. I'll never be able to repay them. My ICU nurses were Traci, Shelly, and Marquita. I did not even know these women and yet they took care of me as if I was family. I cry just thinking about it. Traci would wash my hair at night and talk to me as if I could talk back. She treated my children like her own and never left my side.

Shelly held my hand one day for three hours while I was getting dialysis. Family couldn't be in the room. I was in pain and lonely and confused and couldn't talk. She held my hand and cried with me as if she had nowhere else in the world to go. I couldn't wait to get the vent out and let them know how much I appreciated them. They treated my family with so much love and respect. I wanted to fight and live to show them their work and dedication to their patients was worth so much more than they knew. I needed them to know they helped me fight through pain and struggles. They had no idea how washing my face and hair and talking me through the night showed how they believed in me. They fought for me. Shelly and Traci helped me fight for myself. They weren't just nurses to me. When the day came I could possibly get the vent out, I was so excited I just tried to calmly keep breathing. Dr. McKinnis came in and was so cute and funny. He reminded me of an athletic Andrew McCarthy. He would lean down and say, "Blink or nod if you can breathe." Dr. McKinnis was so supportive of what I needed and yet very cautious to make sure he could heal my lungs back to life. He did an x-ray and checked my breathing and decided he could take the vent out. I wanted to scream with excitement! Did this mean I was getting better? As much faith that I had I wasn't going to die, I never knew if I was going to get better. If you know me at all, you know that not *talking* would be almost impossible for me. I needed it out to get better, to talk to my kids and tell them I love them, to tell Michael thank you for carrying me through all of this.

My family was so nervous. If the doctors took out the vent and I couldn't breathe, I would have to have a trache. If they took it out and I could breathe on my own but my heart couldn't handle the stress, I could have another heart attack. I didn't remember anything I went through before this but Michael *never* stopped saying, "Relax. Don't cry. Don't get upset. Just relax."

I'd blink and nod and try to write him notes and he'd tell everyone, "Just smile at her. Tell her she's doing great and tell her to stay calm." At this point, I didn't know why everyone was a little panicked but I just wanted it out. It was so very hard to stay calm and concentrate so precisely on breathing. Dr. McKinnis smiled and said, "Okay. You want it out?" Tears ran down the side of my face as I nodded yes.

The nurses had given me the entire lesson on how to breathe when they took it out. I was so excited but I knew how calm I needed to be so when they pulled that huge snake out of my throat I didn't fall apart and die again. They came in, told me to relax, and pulled it out. Just for a second, I was scared. Just for that moment, I thought my lungs were going to close up again. I could feel my heart beating through my chest. The doctors and nurses said not to talk for the first few hours. My throat was extremely sore and raw. I wanted to scream to the world. I wanted to jump out of bed and scream, "I can talk. I can talk!"

Getting the vent out gave me an opportunity not just to tell the doctors and nurses my appreciation but for me to let them know exactly what I was dealing with and where my pain was at. Up to this point, Michael was the only one who really understood what I was saying. Now everyone would know how grateful I was to them and when I was in pain.

Having the vent out meant I could look at my kids and tell them I love them. I could tell my family I love them and thank them for never leaving my side. I could laugh and smile and tell Shelly thank you for holding my hand. I could tell Traci thank you for smiling and giving me hope and letting me have a popsicle. And let me tell you, that popsicle was the greatest thing I'd ever tasted.

Having the vent out meant I could try to heal and try to find out why this happened. As lost as I was about what was going on, being in the moment of breathing on my own, I gained back a little hope that I would get better. It gave me a little more control in what was happening. At least I thought so. After what I'd been through, I knew God was in control and giving me my life back little by little, as I was ready to remember it.

The doctors had decided it was time for me to move out of ICU and into a real room. Marquita, one of my ICU nurses, knew that I would be able to do it. I cried to her and said I didn't think I was ready. I knew I was awake, but all of this felt like a dream. I didn't know if it was day or night. When I was awake, I wasn't sure that I wasn't just dreaming. I remember faces and feelings. Different moments of love and peace mixed with confusion and questions. I knew moving me into a real room and out of ICU took a while. They had sit me up and tried to have me eat real food for the first time. My dad went and got me Mexican food since that was my favorite. I couldn't eat it. I felt bad; it was just everything tasted like metal, and it was gross. The nurses said that was normal since I had a vent in for so long and from all the medication. They also had to take me for some final tests before I could be moved. Some sort of brain scan I had to have and couldn't move at all for a few hours. Of course these really cute girls came in to give me the test. It's amazing as a woman, even in the darkest hours of life and death, for some reason, I was still worried about how I looked. I wasn't supposed to move or talk, and yet I wanted to yell out to these adorable young girls, "Hey, I'm not always this bloated!" or "You know, you should never smoke! I used to be small and cute too!" I came out of the test, and I just cried.

Marquita said, "What's the matter? You are ready. Your family is so excited." I felt bad. I just was so scared. In the ICU, I was safe—there was no way I could handle doing anything on my own. Marquita looked at me and said, "You can do it…you will do it." I didn't agree with her, and later, I learned she was right. When they moved me, my family had a little party in my new "real room." The premier of *Big Brother* was on, and Debi was making her famous Mexican casserole and coconut cake. Michael and the kids seemed relieved. My dad was so excited! He loved *Big Brother*, and he loved Debi's coconut cake. My entire family had always watched *Big Brother* together, so it just seemed perfect that the day I moved was also the day it premiered. I wanted so badly to enjoy it with them. Once again, I couldn't eat anything, and the TV was still very blurry. I just wasn't feeling well.

Although I was always happy to be alive, I did have my share of bad days. I was still not sure of what to feel. I was probably more humbled than anything. On this particularly tough day, I was in pain. We didn't know, but Brother Todd was in New Mexico with Jamy and his kids. He had not been to the hospital yet. Kris Steele and Pastor Marc always came, but Brother Todd had not been. We knew he would've been there that first day, so assumed he was on a summer break. On this morning, I wasn't feeling well. My mom was out in the hall. Mike and Debi were watching the Zimmerman trial. My dad was playing cards with Kenzie, as they did a lot. Michael and Bauer had gone down to the cafeteria and the girls were with me. You have to understand, sitting there every day some twelve hours, some twenty-four hours, was something they all *did*, no matter how long or how difficult. Grandmommy, Melisa Kim, and my mom drove the girls back and forth to wash clothes and see the dog. My dad would bring food, and Mike and Debi would take Bauer to see his friends sometimes so he could have a break. My brother kept my dog, and my neighbors mowed our lawn. Kelli and Nicki, Summer, Angie, Melisa, Kim, and Jennifer, our brothers and sisters. Tracy and Terrie, the girls' friends, Harly, Chris, Bryce, Luke and Brandon. They all stayed nights and never left.

Doctors would come over from other parts of the hospital just to pray with me. Nurses brought me icees and limeades, when allowed. I *had* to get better. Too many people were fighting for me. On this particular day though, for some reason, I guess I needed a little extra push. The smallest things would make me emotional and then I had a hard time breathing. I couldn't use my hand. That was hard. My body looked deformed and I had no strength. That was hard. Everything seemed hard.

In the hall, from around the corner, walked in Brother Todd. My mother just broke down crying. She said, "Oh. I knew you'd come today. She needs you." I'm sure he had no idea what she was talking about, but he smiled. Ironically, he'd been in New Mexico on vacation and was now here to pray and talk with me. He helped me have some comfort in the fact I was blessed to be alive.

He said, "What happened?"

I said, "I haven't taken care of myself. I never stopped to breathe, pun intended. Haha."

He said, "You will now."

"Uhh, yes."

My first breath wasn't just about getting that ventilator out and breathing on my own. It wasn't about moving into a real room. It stood for my new breath—the first breath of a second chance. I had to remember that. With every day and night that passed, I had a new fight. I knew from my body what I'd been through, but my mind was healing also. God and my family and friends were doing the fighting for me, but I finally took a breath.

Room 3 North 12

And Jesus answered him, "What I am doing you do not know now, but afterward you will understand."

—John 13:7 (ESV)

Lying in the bed staring at the ceiling trusting strangers with your life is not very easy. You stay calm and remember that you're breathing. It is still tough. From the moment I made it to OKC, I have been on dialysis. Honestly, before I got sick, I didn't know what dialysis was. I'd heard of it. I thought it was for people who needed kidneys or old people. I had no idea what it was for or that one day I would ever need it. Dr. Baluja, as you know, is my kidney doctor. He would come in every day and let me know my numbers and if my kidneys were separating the toxins yet. He was a *rock* for me. He would send me to dialysis and it would scare me to death. When I was in ICU, the machines and Johny and David would come to me. When I was in a real room, they would take the fans off of my bed and wheel me down to the dialysis room. I was on dialysis almost every day for weeks. The clinical definition of dialysis is the purification of blood by dialysis as a substitute for the normal function of the kidneys. Basically, it separated the toxins from the good stuff and flushes it out. From the moment my kidneys shut down, I needed dialysis. It takes hours. I'm not sure how other people handle it, but it made me sick. I mean really sick. When I was in ICU, I was glad when James and the machine came in. I knew my family knew they had a four- to six-hour break. They weren't allowed in so they could sleep or eat and not feel guilty about leaving my bedside. For me, it was pure hell. Especially when I was on the vent. When you think of being physically and mentally in the worst pain you could imagine, I don't know if you could go to the place I was at. I literally had to concentrate every second of every breath I took or I would stop breathing.

I would turn my head to the left so I could see the machine, but I had no idea what it was doing. All the wires were hooked up to my central line. I had so many. The central line was hooked to my neck and the wires went down into my heart and lungs. It's amazing how you can feel so spiritually disconnected from your body and yet such a slave to the pain of it. I remember one of the very first times I had dialysis, I was trying to tell him that I couldn't breathe. I was so upset because he wasn't paying attention to me. I realized later that they're not really supposed to talk to me. At least that's how it started. I don't know how I came to be close to these people but it was as if they wanted to help me. It wasn't their job to be nice to me, but were. They really *didn't* even have to speak to me. David would bring me a blanket when I was cold. He'd have them bring me medicine to help the pain. One afternoon, he could tell I was struggling. He did all he could to get my mind off of it. I was really, really dizzy and nauseous. The doctors were always trying to figure out what was wrong with me. It seemed like every day it was something new. I scared them. The nurses were always afraid at any minute I was going to die. David was very casual. He would tell jokes and talk about his family. He asked me questions about my kids and say how nice my husband was. He told me one day that I would be okay. He was pulling for me. The day I was really sick, he brought me water and some graham crackers. To me, it tasted *so* good. I guess my point is, he didn't even know me, and yet he cared. Dr. Kumar, Johny, David, they had *so* many patients and they didn't have to talk to me like I mattered. I've always known human contact and looking people in the eye mattered. I've tried to teach my kids that relationships are important and people need to matter but I had never been in such a vulnerable position. I had never in my life relied so much on total strangers. I needed these people, not just to physically take care of me, but mentally to help me. And they did.

My daughter Jordan drew a picture in her journal of my room number when I was in ICU. Every time I look at it, I can't help but think about the ceiling tiles. The voices that came on both sides. The nurses holding my hands and washing my hair and celebrating my milestones with me. The sound of the curtain that acts as a door. Knowing my family had sat in those wood chairs for days that turned into weeks. The machine that hits the wall to clean the floors. The feeling of my kids and family touching my arm and my legs and also feeling nothing at all. The sounds and beeps of all the machines.

I think of David sitting there with me for hours and hours. He'd tell a joke and make me laugh. He put my family at ease. He wasn't just doing his job. He was an angel. They all were. I felt like God put them all there because they were the very best and they helped save me. It's still hard to believe how many miracles I experienced on a daily basis. All given by God but accomplished through ordinary people. I heard once that God doesn't call the equipped. He equips the called. These ordinary people-to me were extraordinary. They save people and help people every day for their job. Now that, my friend, is a purpose.

Sideways Kathie Lee and Hoda

Thou hast put more joy in my heart than they have when their grain and wine abound.

—Psalm 4:7 (rsv)

With all three of my kids, I stayed home when they were little. Back then, -when my girls were babies, -Katie was on at 7:00 AM, Kathie Lee was on with Regis, Hoda was on Traci, and Kelly was Hayley on *All My Children*. Well, years have gone by but I still watch all of them.

While in ICU and still on the ventilator, I saw everything sideways. Of couse at the time, I had no ida why and didn't really care. I was so happy to be seeing anything at all and to be awake it didn't really matter to me. I found out later it was because of the stroke. At this time, I didn't even know yet I'd had a stroke. I had some very small brain damage from that. In fact, I remember the night a nurse came in from MRI and said, "We need to take her in for an MRI." Being in the hospital is a little like being on a movie set. Hurry up and wait. Hurry up and get me to the test and then wait for an hour for the procedure to actually happen. I remember my nurse Traci kept coming in and trying to calm me down. There's nothing like being claustrophobic and on a ventilator and going in for an MRI. Traci knew how to keep me calm but wow! I closed my eyes and imagined where I had been. That peace and beauty was soothing to my brain. Traci would say, "Think of something that makes you happy." I kept imagining my kids and Michael outside, all of us together, playing ball and goofing around. I was strong and I could laugh and breathe. Luckily, I got through the MRI without loosing what was left of my sanity. It was nighttime outside, in the real world. I had my days and nights mixed up. The nurse would come in to get my blood and then I could never go back to sleep. The brain damage affected my vision. Every time I opened my eyes it all looked very narrow and upside down. So here I was awake all night and trying to adjust my head so I could see better. If I leaned my head to the right and closed my right eye, it helped. From the moment I opened my eyes, I watched that TV. It wasn't a flat screen or a huge 50-inch but it was a way to look into what was happening outside this itty bitty hospital room.

Different nurses would come in all through the day and night and I never slept. Some I knew well, some I'd never seen before. They would check my weight, heart rate, oxygen levels, hand, feet, central lines, and take my blood. They would always smile but try and be quiet because my family was always asleep next to me. I wasn't at the Ritz, and I didn't have a remote for the TV, but I was so glad it was on Channel 4 through the night. Kathie Lee and Hoda would come on and it took me away from everything that was happening to me. I know it sounds silly but I could not wait for them to come on in the middle of the night. I watched them during the day too but at night it was different. There's something about the middle of the night when everything has stopped. The world is shut down and you just lay there and think about where you've been and what you've woken up to. I couldn't wait to watch them on TV. They were an outlet to the real world for me. I kind of missed the world outside. Not being able to move or breathe, laughing to Kathie Lee and Hoda was such a highlight of my night. In pain on dialysis and not breathing well, laughing to these ladies took me away from all reality but back into it at the same time. I felt like they were on TV just to help me. Only to take me away for one hour. I couldn't sit up or eat, but I could laugh like crazy at Kathie Lee and Hoda. Hoda always has a song she plays for her "favorite of that week," I guess, and Kathie Lee always hates it. When I fell asleep the song of the summer was "Cruise" by Florida Georgia Line. When I woke up it was the guy off *Growing Pains*. Oh wait a minute. Why was he on the Today show? Singing? Maybe it was the son of the guy off *Growing Pains*. Okay, I just loved how they always disagree about music and laugh at each other's stories. Hoda loves Blake Shelton and Kathy Lee doesn't even know what he sings. I wanted them to be my friends. Because I didn't know if it was day or night and I'd usually seen this episode because it was always a replay of the day before. I always enjoyed watching it again because of the time I couldn't remember it anyway. Most of those difficult nights, no one could communicate to me because I was on the ventilator so I always felt like Kathie Lee and Hoda were speaking to me. Deep down, I knew they weren't, but lying there, just us in that little box of my sideways eyesight, they took me out of my hospital world and got me through the night. They didn't even know they were doing it. I'd wake up at one or two in the morning and think it was daytime just to watch them. No one would tell me any differently. You see, Kathie Lee and Hoda weren't worried about upsetting me. They didn't pretend I was okay or I was beautiful, they just made me laugh. No one could understand me or hear me but they didn't have to. They just made me smile on the inside. I knew no matter what they would be on TV the same time day and night and I would laugh and I would feel safe. Since I've woken up, Natalie has been on the entire time in London, waiting on the birth of the prince, and loved so much watching Rachel cook all her amazing recepies, but the laughter and friendship between Kathy Lee and Hoda was such security for me to watch. It did remind me of the relationships I have will all the females in my life. My girls, my mom, and all my friends. Even though it was sideways, their voices were *so* familiar to me and watching them sideways to the right made me feel calm. I loved the two ladies' differences and their closeness together. They could be honest and laugh at each other. I couldn't wait to see what they were going to talk about each day.

When someone is dealing with the magnitude of life and death like I was, all the confusion and the hope and the doubt, plus peace and faith in what had happened, that I still couldn't wrap my brain around, where I'd been and the pain I was dealing with now, laughing at those two ladies was such an escape and a hopeful hour for me. It gave all my people a break from having to make sure I was okay for an hour. I'd forget where I was and just in that one hour of laughter was *normalcy*.

Kathie Lee's Friday funny jokes were so bad I'd laugh. You know even now, even a year later, I wake up in the middle of the night, lean to the left, close the right eye, and watch Kathie and Hoda. I watch them everyday but there's something about watching them in the middle of the night that feels so safe to me. I never thought daytime TV would be the same without Regis or Oprah, but Kathie Lee and Hoda give me peace and a good laugh!

Laughter is healing. It's such an amazing feeling to know joy with pain. Sometimes I cry while I laugh. It's nice to not worry about anything and just laugh. And when they came on TV, I turn my head sideways and forget about what I was going through for at least an hour.

You Still Are

Faith makes us sure of what we hope for and gives us proof of
what we cannot see.

—Hebrews 11:1 (CEV)

My first thought about what I was dealing with at this time was, *Are
you kidding me? I survived death-met Jesus, found "calm," came back to
my family, and now I have to persevere through this excruciating pain and
continue to fight for my life?* I don't mean to sound ungrateful. I was
just so confused. I think I was starting to lack hope. Do you know the
definition of *persevere*? It is to continue in a course of action even in
the face of difficulty with little or no prospect of success. So maybe
I shouldn't use the word persevere. I would succeed. I didn't have a
choice. I was just irritated about it. Where was this pain and struggle
taking me? I didn't really understand. It's hard to explain being so
grateful, confused, and frustrated at the same time. You know you'd
think God had done enough, then walked in Sunshine. She was one
of my nurses but her name fit her perfectly. She brought sunshine to
my mom, Jordan, Raegan, Michael, and Bauer's day. She was awesome!
She would come in and somehow take our minds off what was going
on. Her son had recently been in a bad accident and she had nursed
him back to health. She was a positive life force that brought a little
"sunshine" into our days. You know I was baffled by the love shown
to me and my family by our friends and the people who know us.
What baffled me even more was the love shown by people who *didn't*
know us.

Sunshine had her own kids and her own issues, but she'd walk in
that room and she really was a ray of sunshine. She made my family

smile. She would check on us when we needed her, and she shared her life with us as if we mattered to her, because we did. This is something that's easy for me to talk about, but I'll never forget when the doctors told me I could take a shower for the first time. Okay, I know it doesn't sound like a big deal, but taking a shower is something most of us take for granted. Just to get out of bed, walk *over* to the bathroom, and get into the shower took what seemed like hours. The water made me nervous. They had to tape up all of my lines that went into my heart and lungs and tape up my IV so nothing got wet. Getting the space boots off, getting taped, and putting hair up was quite an ordeal. I had *so* much hair and it hadn't really been brushed in weeks. The sound of the water when Sunshine turned it on scared me. I thought, *She doesn't get paid enough to help me do this.* I cried and cried. My bones were still healing and I still had all the wires. My body was still *so* swollen from everything that happened. All the meds and the massive trauma were not easy on my body. I thought, *Wow. I'll never look the same.* My body looked deformed. Believe me, I'm not vain but that's tough as a woman to come to grips with.

As scared as I was, when the water hit my skin, it was almost as if I was back in that pond with Jesus. I'd been craving *water* ever since and it felt wonderful. I asked Sunshine to go, not because I was shy, but because I needed to cry. I needed to be alone. This was an amazing feat I'd accomplished. I was standing up showering and I wanted to "soak" in every second, pun intended. It's crazy how I went from a normal person to a person feeling accomplished just being alive and taking a shower on my own. I started to get really, really upset and overwhelmed by all of the different emotions. My legs started to feel like they were going to collapse out from under me. Even holding onto the bars, I was scared of falling down. When you lay in bed for a long time, they put Velcro wraps around your legs and they basically massage your legs and feet nonstop. It is to keep you from getting blood clots in your legs. The girls wittingly named them my "space boots." Mainly because that's what they looked like. Every time I needed to get up and go to the bathroom, which took forever, since I could hardly move, the girls had to wake up to take them off.

I felt so sad and helpless. I was the mom. I was supposed to be taking care of them. It just didn't seem right. One morning I was really frustrated and sad. Then walked in Dr. Baluja. You have to remember, at the beginning of this marathon, he didn't really look anyone in the eye. He didn't invest much time in me at Shawnee. I was supposed to die, and he probably didn't see much hope. He didn't really talk to anyone until a few weeks after I actually survived. Don't get me wrong, he was there and was an amazing doctor. He just didn't get too close. At first he probably didn't want to invest too much, but after I lived and he saw me fight, I gained his respect. He believed in me from that moment on. I mean, he'd had real patients who needed attention and I wasn't even awake and on dialysis. As the weeks went on, Dr. Baluja and Dr. Blair came into my room every day. So did Dr. McKinnis and Dr. Cheema and Dr. Kumar, but the main concern was kidneys at this point and Dr. Blair never left so those were the two I spent the most time with. In the beginning, Dr. Baluja would come in, tell me the numbers had not changed, no urine, and he'd leave. Then when I got the vent out and seeing that I was a fighter, and the more he was around my family he got to know them and me and on a daily basis, we just grew closer and created a bond and he began to fight with us. The relationship I had with those two men—Dr. Baluja and Dr. Greg Blair—was like no other I could ever explain. Greg and I have a past of loving each other's children, sharing the death of Anne, and creating this amazing friendship with his new wife Jenn. We started with a bond. Dr. Baluja didn't know us but what you create from weeks and weeks in a hospital, to me, equals years out in the real world.

They both held my life in their hands and Sunshine held my pride and mental health in hers, and yet it was as if we were all teaching each other. Day after day, Dr. Baluja would walk in and I'd ask, "Any changes?" and he'd shake his head no. You see, I needed my numbers to change. Most peoples' kidney numbers function at 0.5 or below. I started out an extremely high number with no function at all for weeks. The earliest number I remember was an 11. Later, my kidneys began working and producing urine but were not separating the toxins and flushing them out. That meant I had to stay on dialysis so the machine could separate the toxins. It wasn't good. I'd go to dialysis and sweet

James would take care of me and then I'd be back to my room. Dr. Baluja would come in the next day, shake his head "no changes," and I would say, "It's okay! Tomorrow it will be!" I tried to always stay positive. I *knew* things would turn around. Dr. Baluja and I would talk and he'd joke around with the kids. He was always very professional, but we started to goof around a lot. Even when I was in pain, I'd give him crap about something. I think he was always surprised about my attitude but he didn't know what I'd seen and experienced.

One day I woke up very early. I wasn't in a good place. Michael and my three kids were all asleep on one cot and a chair next to my bed. Even though they had a room, they rarely left my side. It had been a tough night wearing the space boots, watching Kathie Lee and Hoda, Duck Dynasty, and not being able to sleep. Michael would always fall asleep in that wood chair with his head cocked to the side and all the kids' legs hanging off the cot or curled up around each other. Dr. Baluja came in this one morning and once again shook his head as if to say "no changes" I got *so* mad. I didn't understand why I was going through *all of this! Still!*

I ripped the Velcro off my space boots and was crying uncontrollably. I acted like I was going to get up but I really couldn't. I felt defeated! "We've been through enough!" I wanted to yell. Dr. Baluja came over to my bed. He said, "Okay." I just looked at him. He continued, "Have your pity party. You deserve it. You've been through a lot. But then stop. Look over here at your family that has *never once* left your side, then get over it. You're lucky to be alive. Who cares about your kidneys? You're alive." I sat there completely dumbfounded. Tears flowed down my face. He was right.

I felt like Dr. Baluja stood for a lot of meaning in all of this. Dr. Blair stood for my *life*, but Dr. Baluja stood for my *fight*. When everything you have had left you, it's a helpless feeling. Pretend for a minute you're not in your home, your job, your car. You can't breathe, you can't talk. Your children and family are devastated, other people dress and shower you. You can't really move or go to the bathroom without help. You have all of your thoughts right at your grasp, but you can't move enough or think enough to reach them. You're relying on people you don't know to care about you and talk to you, to medicate you and help your pain.

Not easy. With Baluja it was. I knew he cared about me and my family. He was fighting too. I knew he wouldn't sleep until I was *well*. The bond and the gratitude I had for these men—and Dr. McKinnis—I cannot put into words. I knew Dr. Blair would fight for my life. I was grateful Dr. Baluja did. For Dr. Baluja to start out disconnected and become such an important part of my recovery cannot be explained. I replied to his scolding with "okay," but I was kind of frustrated when he said that, as much as I cared about what he said, I thought, *What?* I wasn't myself, and I was afraid I never would be again.

He continued, "I watched you those first days. You're a fighter. Keep fighting."

I was crying. He was right. I was still Julie. I said, "Well, you know how to put a girl in her place." I was so grateful to be alive for my family, but I was tired. My back hurt and my space boots drove me crazy. I was starving and I wanted to be able to walk and think without being confused, and blurry visions bouncing round in my head. I wasn't trying to be ungrateful, I was just trying to hang on. I felt out of control. Dr. Baluja was such a medical straightforward guy. He wasn't the kind of doctor I would have expected to shake me up. I looked at him with tears. "I wish you'd known me before. I was feisty and loud and I was kinda funny."

We both softly laughed and he said, "Oh, you still are."

As the weeks went on, Michael and I grew closer and closer to Dr. Baluja. They would team up against me and make me drink those awful shakes so I'd gain weight. Jesus didn't promise my days would be easy and maybe I did have some fight left.

I believe God sent all of these people into my recovery to teach me something. I just had to be willing to learn it. Sunshine lived up to her name and Baluja gave me some fight back. I learned in those weeks to hang on. No matter what my body went through, you have to dig deep and find within yourself what *you still are*.

Downtown Lights

I took my troubles to the Lord;
I cried out to him, and he answered my prayers.

—Psalm 120:1 (NLT)

The crazy thing about what was happening to me was that I never felt like I wasn't going to live. Waking up, I had no idea the pain I was about to endure, but I knew it wasn't my time to die. I didn't know why but I woke up to the fight of my life, and not one ounce of strength. How was I supposed to fight? I could barely move. I couldn't see unless I cocked my head to the right, and most everything was blurry. My left hand looked like a black softball glove. My body was swollen and shut down. My chest bones still felt like glass. Bauer kept telling me my eyes looked "full of blood." I had more belief in God than anyone, but where was my *faith*? When I woke up I had so much gratitude to be alive and never digested what really happened. Then I started finding out. A little more each day and I couldn't wrap my brain around it. Somewhere between the central lines and the x-rays, I was tired. I had MRIs and EKGs, nausea, pneumonia, a VRE infection that meant no one could really touch me. I was given blood and on dialysis and being positive and trying to stay in that place of peace. It took fifteen minutes to get up and walk to bathroom, and I always had help. Rachel had brought me some soft, comfy pajamas to wear, so I would feal normal. I couldn't wear them because of the central lines and the IV. I so desperately needed to get back to my calm. I really wanted to scream out, "Are you kidding me!" I can't do this. This is harder than before. "Why did you bring me back to go through this?"

I remember laying there in *so* much pain and I had a lot of visitors come in and out every day. My friends and family waited hours some days just to see me for a few minutes. I wanted so badly to smile and be so grateful, because I *was* and I needed to see all these people. It helped me so very much to see them and talk, but it was hard. One day, I remember I had just gotten back into my room. All of my friends and family would sit in the waiting room and wait to see me or just sleep and sit out there for hours every day. They would wheel me by the waiting area to go to tests and dialysis and back and I would wave. Kathy L. came in on this particular day and sat by my bed. She said, "God saved you for a reason. He must have big plans for you." Tears just rolled down her face. "So many people love you, Julie. This is because of who you are. People are praying and fighting for you to live." I just cried. I needed to hear that. It gave me strength.

Phyllis and Kaily came in with Melisa and Phyllis said, "If you ever doubted your husband loved you, you can't now."

Melisa said, "Your parents and family own that waiting room! Everyone is playing cards and bringing food." After weeks of being here, we still had so much support. My neighbors were mowing my lawn, and Don's Plants came every week and took care of all of my flowers. Steve at the bank was taking care of our accounts, so Michael didn't have to worry about that kind of stuff and was able to focus on my recovery.

Even the nurses brought brownies and doctors from all over the hospital would come into my room and ask if they could pray with us. People and doctors who didn't even know us. They'd say, "We've heard your story and we were wondering if we could pray with you?" I knew what was going on was *too big* to wrap my brain around at the time.

That night after all the visitors and procedures, I had the nurse give me a pain pill so I could get some good rest. Nights were tough and I was in pain. I fell asleep and I had the most incredible dream.

Some might say it was the medicine. I think it was God again. Whatever it was, I saw the most vivid images. It was a dream but yet it was so very real.

Michael was grinning and he was laughing. Jordan and Raegan were wrestling on my bed in their pink matching pajamas with Cinderella on in the background. I kept hearing Bauer's laugh. Sitting at the kitchen table doing homework with Bauer, telling him to stop throwing the baseball. Hearing the girls say, "Mom, we love you more than the whole universe." "Mom, Bauer hit me!" The vision of Michael on the baseball field throwing his hands up at an umpire. Looking at our parents' faces of relief when I woke up. And then I saw it again. My place of peace with Jesus. Only he wasn't there anymore. I was there alone, just the two canoes and me with calm water. It scared me. I woke up with a short squeal, sweating and in a panic. I sat up. Took my space boots off by myself and stood. I looked at my family, my husband, girls, and son all very uncomfortably asleep. They had lied there like that for so long. My family and friends had never left the waiting rooms. They stopped their entire lives because my life stopped. I was overwhelmed, and humbled. I had so many things left to say to them. So many things I had left to do with my life! I scooted over to the window. I'd seen these downtown lights so many times in my life yet today they were different. I felt like George Bailey and I cried out to God, "I am sorry. I've been so wrong. I just want to live. Please let me live. I'm so sorry." You see, at that moment, I had realized that peace wasn't a place. Peace wasn't a feeling.

Peace was faith.

God wasn't trying to teach me *not to die*, he was trying to teach me *how to live*. Living wasn't just about breathing. The fight wasn't in what was wrong with my body. The fight was what was wrong with my heart and my head. I decided right then, as I looked out at the downtown lights, that I was gonna fight for my family and my life, but the fight within myself was over.

I was alive. I could watch *Psych* and *Castle* with Bauer. I could help the girls with friend and boy issues. I was here to tell Michael and my family I loved them. I could see my friends and laugh with them and they knew I loved them. I would fight to get better for them, but my fight to *heal*, my fight with *myself*, my fight with *God*, was over. *I gave it all to him* and the craziest thing happened. I started to get better. Every day I got better.

Independence Day

These things I have spoke unto you, that in me ye might have peace.
In the world ye shall have tribulaton;
but be of good cheer;
I have overcome the world.

—John 16:33 (KJV)

July 4

I woke up differently that next morning and every morning after that. I appreciated every breath I took and every single person who walked into that room. It's not that I didn't before—I did. I just quit worrying and fighting and decided to live. I lived in a hospital room and drank diabetic shakes, but I was alive.

The day the physical therapist came in was a big step for me. Literally. The first day she came in, I really didn't want to get out of bed and try to walk. I was very comfortable lying there and scooting to the bathroom or the window. My bones weren't completely healed yet and I had *zero* balance. I really can't explain what trying to walk was like. The sweet therapist wrapped a huge belt around my waist. Michael called it my seatbelt. She could hold onto me that way in case I fell. Which the first few times, I almost did. I couldn't balance, I'd almost fall forward or get going too fast. It was kind of funny actually. Michael would make me get up every day and walk. Each time, I could go a little further and walk a little smoother. Some days I did not want to go. That trip around the hospital floor felt like a 5K marathon. No matter how I felt or if I was too tired, I would go walk, and each week, I would get a little sturdier and balance a little bit better. I remember the first day I walked from my room to the waiting room.

Inside I kind of felt like a small toddler. Everyone was standing up in the waiting room clapping, almost as if it were my first time to ever walk. There was a lot of joy that day. I even walked back to the room myself.

My family stood next to me so I didn't fall, but I was doing it on my own. I was proud to have conquered the next step. Another milestone in my recovery.

For days I was hoping to get to go outside. On the Fourth of July most people are looking forward to hamburgers, hot dogs, a swimming pool, and fireworks. Me, I was hoping for fresh air. I would stare out that hospital window day and night and the thought of fresh air against my face seemed so healing and freeing. Dr. Greg had hinted maybe I could be wheeled outside to see the fireworks. I was trying not to get my hopes up. I wasn't even sure if I would be physically able to handle it, but I didn't care. Breathing in fresh air and a breeze blowing on my skin would do more good for me mentally than trying to get outside would strain me physically. I didn't really understand it before when I would hear people say "the power of prayer" and "power of love in healing." You think you know. You think you understand, but unless you've experienced it you cannot comprehend what it means. I'm still trying to wrap my brain around it and it happening to me. You feel some sort of spiritual power force when you know entire towns are praying for you. People that didn't even know me were praying for me. My family and friends and churches were willing me to live. Up to that point, I'd been angry and resentful about so many things in my life. Since letting it all go and truly embracing what was right in front of me, I felt a weight had been lifted.

When Dr. Greg came in that night and told us I would be able to go outside, I was so excited. It was a new day. Possibly the beginning of my healing. It was Raegan's night to stay. Jordan and Bauer were in Shawnee with our families, so Michael got a wheelchair and the three of us began on our journey.

It sounds silly to call it a journey, but that's exactly what it was. I felt like we were setting out on an adventure, and I was a giddy child.

We started down the hall. I was in a wheelchair, and Michael was pushing me. It was later into the evening. The hospital halls were bare and it was somewhat calm. It was funny. We kind of felt like we were "escaping." Even though we had permission, it kind of felt like we were sneaking out and it made it even more exciting. We headed down the elevator and down the front entrance. You can imagine my anticipation? Raegan and Michael were excited too. My entire memory of this hospital up to this point consisted of square ceiling tiles and lights in every other one. I've just started sitting up and trying to walk so being in a wheelchair and getting to go through the hospital with my own eyes was amazing. I felt like a human being again. As we got closer to the front door, I could see the breeze blowing the flowers and it seemed as if real life was just a few steps away. As we approached the sliding front doors of the hospital entrance, we realized they were locked. They wouldn't open, since it was after hours. What? We all just started laughing. So we traveled back through the halls of the hospital and realized we'd have to go out through the emergency room if we wanted to get outside. I was like a small child on my way to see Santa Claus. I was so happy!

Going through the ER was a little scary, but this whole night felt daring so it made it even more fun. Those doors opened, and we got outside and the air hit me in the face. I felt renewed. Once out there, we realized we were on the opposite side of the hospital and we wouldn't be able to see the Bricktown fireworks show. We had to go all the way around the outside of the hospital. It was so fun. Michael was pushing me and part of it was downhill and it seemed like we were going really fast! In that moment, I felt the very best I'd ever felt in my life. I was yelling out with laughter and pure joy. The fresh July air filled my lungs and my skin and my soul. There's no way to describe the safety and security I felt and yet so free at the same time. Raegan was laughing. Michael was trying not to lose the wheelchair. It was real. It was happiness.

To me, breathing that air in stood for freedom. Literally.

Walking the floor of the hospital that week and feeling pure joy. Going outside. Laughing.

I felt human again. It was Independence Day. It was my Independence Day. The irony of the air and freedom.

The irony of downtown lights and the fireworks.

I was in search of life, and I was finding it in places it had always been.

Bauer's Summer Apartment

If I speak in the tongues of men and of angels, but have not love, I am a noisy gong or a clanging cymbal. And if I have prophetic powers, and understanding all mysteries and all knowledge, and if I have all faith, so as to remove mountains, but have not love, I am nothing. If I give away all I have, and if I deliver my body to be burned, but have not love, I gain nothing.

So faith, hope, love abide, these three; but the greatest of these is love.

—1 Corinthians 13:1–3 and 13 (RSV)

I'll never forget the day we found out Bauer was a boy. We were all very excited. After having twin girls, I wasn't sure if I knew how to handle a boy. I did know we were ready and grateful to have our son. He was our sweet baby who twisted my ring to fall asleep and that would not sleep in his bed. The girls lived to mother him and every time they'd talk to him he'd just goo goo and giggle. Fast forward ten years, all he and Jordan did was fight and when you'd ask him what he was doing he'd say, "Being awesome!" I was still trying to figure out how to handle a boy but I loved every second of it. When he was about four years old, we started this sweet thing where I'd say, "I love you more than the whole world," and he'd say, "The universe is bigger." I'd spread my arms open wide and I'd say, "More than the whole universe." We'd laugh and hug tight. He'd hold his arms up and say, "Hode choo. Hode choo," meaning *hold you*. My heart would melt. He had Michael and the girls wrapped around his finger too, not to mention all of our parents.

My job as a parent is always to make sure my children feel safe and know they're loved. No matter what happens in my life, if I've raised heart-healthy children who know Jesus and love people, I will feel like I did my job. Of course, you don't wanna screw them up *either*!

Normally fathers always have a bond with their sons. Bauer and Michael do. They always have. Michael has always coached Bauer and they fish and watch sports together. They are great together, but he always had a special bond with me too.

Bauer is my baby so he and I have always been close when he needed his momma. When he was tired and wanted to go to sleep he would reach for me and say, "Hode you, hode you." I'd pick him up and he'd twist my ring with his fingers until he'd fall asleep. I loved rocking him to sleep and feeding him his favorite pasta from Chili's. He was so spirited and loved watching his sisters. Every day when Jordan and Raegan would go to school, he would go in their room and take all of their clothes out of all of their drawers and throw them all over the room.

Every day they would come home from school. They'd run in from getting off the bus and go into their room and scream, "Bauer!" Bauer and I would just hide and laugh. They'd run in and wrestle him. It wasn't soon after that I started working again and the older Bauer got, the busier he got with activities and school. He loved sports so much and Michael took him since he coached. No matter what was going on, Bauer and I always found certain things that he and I just shared. I know to always stay very close to him I needed to make sure we spent time together and cared about something that he and I shared that had nothing to do with anyone or anything else. On the way to school every morning, we'd sing a song called "Good Morning," by Mandisa. Bauer is kind of quiet. He's kind of like his dad in the way he doesn't say too much, but he's very witty and funny and he has certain ways he shows love. Every day he got in the car, he'd turn on that song and we'd sing and laugh. I knew that was the same thing as saying, "I love you, Mom." I'd sing and embarrass him and say, "I love you, Bauer." He'd roll his eyes and say, "Okay, okay." But I knew when he looked at me he meant I love you with that smile and singing our song. We also always watched *Castle* and *Psych* together no matter what. He'd run in from practice and say, "I'm here," and we'd lay on the floor and watch both shows on Monday and Wednesday night. We didn't have much special time. We were on such a routine with practices and school. I cherished those Monday and Wednesday night shows we watched together.

Sometimes as a parent we feel invisible. We wash their clothes and get their uniforms ready. We make their lunches and do their homework with them. It's kind of like kids don't realize who has all their stuff in place and ready to go every day. They don't think about how those clean folded clothes got in their drawers or how their uniform and Gatorade is ready at the door. And that's fine. They're not supposed to know or even think about it. That's my job. Kids are only supposed to worry about their schoolwork and if their friends can hang out.

The day I died, everything changed. I can't *imagine* what Bauer went through standing in the ICU room and having to say good-bye to his mother. Sitting in the waiting room and hearing, "Code blue. Code blue." And the alarm sounding off knowing it was his mother. Not just once, but *four* times. I know after the third time Michael had him go in and talk to me. "Tell your mom you love her," he told him. Bauer didn't say a word after that for a while. After I woke up and lived, he was still very quiet. To me, sometimes, silence is the loudest sound and I was worried about *him*.

After I was moved from ICU, he was still very cautious with me. I knew he had never left here. In fact, when I first got very sick, my friend Carol looked in to our family having a room here at the hospital. Carol researched it and my dad went and set it up. It was a room in a wing of the hospital where families stayed while their loved ones were in the hospital. Bauer called it his "summer apartment." We were of course downtown and had a great view. His best friend Langston stayed with him so he wasn't alone. Jason, Michael's friend and Melisa's brother, gave him a PSP and an Xbox to put in the room so Bauer wasn't so bored and could take his mind off of things. So many of his friends came to see him and he'd say, "Hey, you wanna stay in my summer apartment?" It would make me smile. I was so worried about Bauer the entire time I was in the hospital. I was concerned how all of this would affect him.

One day he was trying to get ready for baseball practice and he couldn't find all of his stuff, and he just yelled out, "Mom usually does all this clothes!" At the same time I felt sad for him I also felt appreciated. I knew he was struggling. Children are not supposed to worry about their parents. I knew he'd seen things that would haunt him forever. One of the first things he said to me was, "Mom, your eyes are full of blood." I didn't know what he meant until I was able to sit up and I asked my mom for a mirror. They were. They looked full of blood. It was from all of the coding and it took weeks to go away, but I knew what he'd seen and experienced and I just kept wondering how I was going to fix this. I just wanted to hold him and take care of him. I didn't want him to be sad and I knew this would change him forever. I loved him more than I would ever be able to show him. Even though so many friends took him to the movies and to swim, there was still a fear in his eyes. His coaches, his friends, and all of our family did everything they could to help his summer seem somewhat normal. I appreciated that so much, but I still knew he needed more.

My hope is he understands now that I'm human, which is what I'm just figuring out. We are all human and extraordinary, and scary, and unexpected situations happen in life. I got sick, but I did get better. I hope we can use this to not only grow closer, but to change his life. I know he loves me and is glad I'm here with him and it may be weeks or months before he's able to discuss what he's really going through, and that's ok. The fact that I'm here to go through it with him, I will forever be grateful. The fact he had a "summer apartment" to escape to, I'm sure he will never forget.

Superman

And if I have all faith, so as to remove mountains, but have not love, I am nothing.

So faith, hope, love abide, these three; but the greatest of these is love.

—1 Corinthians 13:2 and 13 (RSV)

When I was a little girl, I loved riding in the car. I'd lay me head against the window and stare up to the sky. The sharp blue behind the white fluffiness almost put me in a trance. We'd drive to Stroud every weekend to see my grandparents and I always looked forward to the sound of the road and the music in the background as I tried to find animal shapes in the sky. Driving to the coffee shop, I'd ask my grandpa, "What's that white line across the sky?" He'd reply, "That's Superman." Deep down, part of me believed him. Those were the years Superman and the beautiful Christopher Reeve were so popular. I'd watch Superman and every time I went outside and saw a white line in the sky, I never thought it was a plane. I believed it was Superman. The thought of marrying a man who could protect and take care of me was kind of unimaginable. I never really wanted to even get married and I always knew I sure didn't need anyone to take care of me. I could take care of myself. I wasn't the kind of girl who wanted babies and the white picket fence, and of course only existed in the movies. Plus, my grandpa and my dad were so good I'd probably never find a Superman who compared. Well, as I've said before, if you want to make God laugh, tell him your plans because he definitely had a different one for me than I had for myself.

Someone once said the secret to their thirty-year marriage was "We never wanted to get a divorce at the same time." After you've been married awhile, you realize how true that statement is—one of us was always fighting for the other one. When Michael and I decided to get married, we looked for rings together. I found the most beautiful princess cut on a platinum band. That was it—that was the one I wanted. The man selling it to us said, "Well, that one is on sale because it has a flaw."

Michael said, "Oh, you don't want one with a flaw in the diamond, do you?" I looked at it, and I still loved it.

I said, "No, I do. The minute I saw it, I knew that was the ring. It was our ring."

Michael said, "Are you sure?"

"That's the ring," I replied. "I don't need a perfect diamond. You and I are flawed—our ring can be too." He didn't argue too much; it was cheaper. Two flawed people trying to love, raise kids, and fight the battle of life.

Sometimes I look at Michael and I know I could not love him anymore than I do now, but my love grows every day. Sadly, when I got sick, I wasn't sure if he even liked me. I didn't really like him. You can love someone but not like them at all. As I've mentioned, we were in a tough place. Our kids were at that crazy age. You wake up early, get everyone fed and ready for school, try to make sure you at least have the same shoes on, work all day, phone calls, emails, bills, dinner, get everyone home, do dinner, change clothes, and run, run, run, whether it's coaching practices, dance, soccer, or church, we would all get home late, watch TV together as a family, do homework, say prayers, and get ready for bed. Most of the time, Michael and I were both putting orders in and just trying to breathe from the day just behind us and anticipating the day ahead. I think when a lot of people get married they are not prepared for what's actually in store for them. Marriage isn't easy. In fact, it's very difficult. There were a few years there that I truly didn't believe that it had anything to do with love. That was until June of 2013. When you say your wedding vows you don't realize you may really have to follow them. When Michael said "in sickness and in health," he probably had no idea what he was getting into.

I didn't know how much he loved me. He probably will never know how much I love and appreciate him. Michael and I have always functioned pretty independently. We weren't one of those couples who needed each other every second. I've always trusted him even though at times I felt like the entire town had all lost their minds around us. For years, people kept getting caught having affairs and leaving their families. I knew Michael would never do that but I always thought it was because of *him*, not because of me. You see, Michael is the kind of man who is very close to God and his faith. He has to look at himself in the mirror and sleep at night. I've never known a more honest human being. He has morals and a conscience. These days, sadly, that is rare in a man. I know he's difficult and stubborn but he's loyal and even if he has a hard time saying I love you, he never lacks in showing it. Well, maybe he did sometimes. Honestly when I got sick I wasn't even sure if he loved me. When I woke up from being "asleep," he was the voice I kept hearing. Michael brought me peace and love. When I realized what he'd actually been through, it took me a while to digest it all. You can describe what they went through and talk about it, but unless you watched it or went through it, you probably can't even imagine it. My problem is I didn't do either one. I didn't watch it or go through it. Everything he and my entire family had to deal with themselves. I was so consumed with where I had been, I didn't want to think about where they had been.

It took me a while to understand, if I even can, what he and my family went through. I know this—he never once left my side. He prayed constantly. He believed in me and my life. He wouldn't let go and he wouldn't for one second listen to anyone say I wasn't going to live. Can you close your eyes and imagine this? Strip yourself of all your life—your home, your clothes, your job, your phone, your dinners out, anything material. You are in a room and it's just you, your kids, your family, and God waiting to see if your spouse, the rest of your life, will live and wake up. Everything that I thought mattered, all the sports and the job, the dancing and bills and laundry and that rut of a routine you thought was so super important, it all stopped.

That summer while we were in the hospital, the new Superman movie was released. The commercial ran constantly. Along with the

Chevy Strong commercial. The music from both of these rang in my head all of the time. That's what Michael was, he was Superman.

Michael and I had been through so much to get to this place. We'd already been through so much. I remember looking at him and saying, "If we can get through *all* of this, we can get through anything." I had no idea. He was so strong. Christopher Reeve was an amazing Superman because he was understated and humble. He wanted to help without taking credit. That was my husband. Our marriage, in the beginning, was tough. I had the best grandpa and dad in the history of the world. I thought every marriage was supposed to be like theirs.It wasn't. It took me a while to figure out that that was okay. We loved each other in the beginning, but life happens so fast and you look up and wonder, "Who is he? And do I even care?" Then in the hospital you find out this quiet man that hardly says I love you never left your side and willed and prayed you back to life. I figured out what shocked me was the constant vigil at my bedside and never once giving up on me. I was so sick and the nurses and doctors told Michael over and over again to say good-bye and let me go and not *one* time did he even consider it. Not once. He didn't change clothes or shower or eat because he didn't want to leave me. I believe in the power of prayer more now than I ever could have believed in anything, but I truly believe Michael was given superpowers through this experience. It was only my family and that hospital bed. In that bed was the person they loved who looked like a stranger. That stranger who wouldn't wake up and looked completely deformed. Never once did they waiver. Never once did he lose faith. Not one time did he leave me. To me that is Superman.

He was everything I needed right at the exact time I needed him. He never broke and he was *so* strong. Love isn't said, it's shown. Shown when it needs to be shown and shown at times when I wasn't paying attention. Just because he didn't show me love the same way I'd grown up seeing my mother shown love didn't mean he didn't love me. I didn't know that. For a while I thought love didn't have anything to do with being married. You look up one day and you're tested. Tested with your vows and real life and you begin to see he does love you.

I never thought I'd be that person that would wonder "Why am I married?" but lying there I didn't just realize how much I loved him but how much I needed him. He was *hard* on me but it pushed me to walk again and eat again and fight to get better.

Over the past years, looking at each other we'd probably rather scratch each other's eyeballs out than kiss. Sometimes I just wanted to punch him when he'd talk. But that's just life. When it came down to it, there was *no one* there better to fight for me.

Waking up and finding out what he did for me, I wasn't surprised but sad at what he and the kids and my family had to go through.

Superman came in all shapes and sizes. Although Christopher Reeves and Chevy are wonderful examples, I believe no one is a better fit for the title than Michael. His love, his faith, *never waivered*. He's dealt with a lot of adversity and although he doesn't do it the way I thought was "right," he does it his way. The strong way. The Superman way—and I wouldn't be *alive* without him. We would joke the nurses liked him. They wanted someone to love them like he loved me. It's funny to think I didn't even know he loved me like that!

Love is shown in different ways and at different times. It's not always when we want it, but it is when we need it. He doesn't wear a cape or fly in the air but he's my Superman and I love him and I'm grateful his powers and strength and faith helped heal me.

Journals Jordan and Raegan

Do nothing from selfishness or conceit,
but in humility count others better tha yourselves.

—Philippians 2:3 (ESV)

From the moment I woke up, I saw my girls' faces. They were there and were strong. It was hard and I try not to think about what they went through. The light I saw in their faces when I woke up is something I'll never forget. The guilt is overwhelming. I am the mother. As I said with Bauer, the mom is supposed to take care of the family, and yet these girls were taking care of me. On a day when most girls would have been asking, "What car will I get?" these two were watching their mother die. Over and over again. It was the night of their sixteenth birthday. They sat at the hospital every single day. They kept journals of everything that happened. It's funny to me how their personalities came out in their journals. Raegan would write daily as if she was talking to me.

"Mom, today you're doing better. Everyone is here. We haven't left your side." She drew pictures of Dumbo and his mom hugging and holding each other. We both share a love for elephants and what other mother/child character showed more love than Dumbo?

Jordan's journal entries were very precise with numbers of how my blood pressure, heart rate, and urine levels were. Jordie would vent to me in her entries about people who had upset her and how sad she was. Where one was so emotional, the other one was so scientific.

Both of them helped me with everything once I was able to move around. They were so patient. They smiled every second and never broke down in front of me. Sleeping in a chair for weeks, they'd wake up every thirty minutes or so and check to make sure I was still breathing.

They'd take off my space boots so I could get up to go to the bathroom. I had to wear them. Especially with all of my blood clots, I was at risk. The boots hooked up to the bed, so if I ever wanted to get up, they had to be taken off. Not fun, but the girls nicknamed them my "space boots." They did kind of look like astronaut boots. Jordan and Raegan always tried to find the positive or funny in all things. They could have been weak. They could have played the victim and tried to make it about them. They didn't. They're not like that. In fact, they are quite the opposite. Yes, at times, they would disappear or go home to get clothes and I know they broke down. But while at the hospital, they were so selfless and joyful. When they'd walk into the room, it was like a ray of light. I remember feeling really strong one day and decided to stand and lift my leg to stretch. Neither one of them—my legs—would go up very far far. The girls would hold on to me, so I wouldn't fall. They tried to show me posts on their phones so I could see the love people were sending. They talked to me all day about Rachel Ray recipes we could make when I got home or what was going on with the *Housewives* series. They knew I loved the *Housewives* and it helped distract me. They would walk across the street and get food or drinks I was craving once I could eat. Everything they *did* was for me or Bauer or their dad. They were taking care of us so selflessly. It was beautiful to watch. I was so proud of them because I knew the pain they were going through and what they'd watched happen to me would stay with them for the rest of their lives. It doesn't seem fair to me that such good girls have to go through that, but I also believe God knew my family, the girls, were strong enough and good enough on the inside to get through whatever happened.

I've seen so much pain and you wonder why do these things happen to the *best* people I know—the Blair girls, the Ricks family, Samantha, and now my family. But yet, if you think about it, really nasty people wouldn't take lessons and trials and turn them into something that matters. God gives us the strength to get through the pain and then the knowledge to reach people with it. Jordan and Raegan have been through much more than most teenage girls their age, but they know more than anyone what matters in life. They appreciate the moments we have together, whether it's a dance competition, a football game, or just sitting in the backyard talking. They were not wrapped up in the car they drive or back-to-school shopping. They were grateful we were all together. They're not perfect—they're kids and they're human—but I am so proud of their pure hearts and love they have for their family and friends.

I remember one of my later days in the hospital. We were leg stretching just to see if I could go any higher. On this day, I did. I lifted my foot up to the top of the bed and we all three squealed with excitement.

I was so proud to have daughters that would rather be lifting my leg and genuinely grateful that I could than be anywhere else in the world. God will do amazing things in their lives and I'm grateful and blessed to call them *mine*.

I always text the girls, "I love love you." Since there's two of them I would write love twice. One day I accidentally typed "I live love you" and from that day on I always typed live love you. We don't just love our children, we live for them and because of them. I never knew how true that text would actually become.

Guacamole and a Turkey Sandwich

Greater love hath no man than this,
that a man lay down his life for hi friends.

—John 15:13 (KJV)

There's something to be said about a friendship that lasts twenty-five years. Not just knowing someone twenty-five years but truly having a friendship. You know the worst and the best of them. You accept them the way they are without judgment but always with criticism and laughter. It's a feeling of safety and truth and not regretting it the next day. Someone who didn't choose to be in your life but did choose to stay. When you're from a small town, we can't always help whom we have to be around or whom we have to see, but we do choose whom we share with, love with, and hope with. I knew she was *a* friend, but until the craziest times of my life, I didn't realize how much she was *my* friend. We all have blessed friendships. I've mentioned many of them while telling my story. My family and friends stayed with me night after night. Sometimes they would wait for hours just to see me for a few minutes. Everyone that loves us brought our kids giftcards and food. They all knew taking care of my family was taking care of me. Michael's friends were there day after day, giving him strength. Some had a hard time seeing me that way, and couldn't come back to the hospital, but I knew they were praying for me and supporting my family. One friendship is not better than the others; they're all different. There was just something so special about this particular night for me.

You know when you're little and all your friends can stay the night? I would get so excited. We had to have plenty of snacks, music, movies, and usually a phone to prank call the boys we liked. Those were the good ole days before caller ID and you could hang up on a boy if you chickened out talking to him. Your only worry in the world was if you and your friends will have enough popcorn. That happy feeling you have inside, free from any real life thoughts. Usually a feeling reserved solely for children. You don't know when you are young, that you may never feel that way again. My brain was still hanging onto my carefree Fourth of July and hanging to the hope of prayer and constant fight that I would heal. Well, this was even a better day than I expected. Dr. Baluja came in and told us that I could come off diet restriction! What!? Really? I hugged him. It had been so difficult and I was so excited!

When I have tried to eat anything, it always tasted like metal so I've had a hard time. Plus, for weeks, I'd been on a diet restriction because of my kidneys. When Chad and Melisa brought Van's carrot cake to the hospital for Michael's birthday and my mom and dad and Michael's mom and dad brought food, it was awful. Angie and the kids were there too. It was so fun, I just couldn't eat. I felt good and was even sitting up. He probably wasn't expecting my crazed excitement, but he got it!

It was Melisa and Raegan's turn to stay up with me. Melisa was coming up in a few hours and I told her I could eat real food! She was excited too so she made me my very favorite food in the whole world— Melisa's guacamole. No one makes guacamole better than Melisa. At this point, I could have eaten salt-free broth and diabetic shakes. Oh wait! That is what I was eating! The thought of fresh guacamole made me giddy like that young girl, and we were going to have our own slumber party.

Michael was always very funny about who stayed with me, of course, family and a few friends. But when it came to Melisa, anything goes. She wasn't just Chad's wife, she had been friends with Michael longer than anyone. She is loyal and caring and listens when she needs and gives advice when asked. That's the thing about our group of girlfriends. We can razz each other and talk about each other, but *no one* else can and we are always there for each other. Just like my family, my friends rarely left the hospital and I know that gave me strength. Strength to fight and laugh and heal.

Melisa and Raegan moved the cot to go right beside my bed and the brown old chair up to the cot. That way it was as if we are all on the same bed chatting and laughing. Of course, I wasn't tired because I was always up all through the night and take my weight and check my urine so the thought of being up late to watch TV, eat guacamole, and laugh with my girls, I definitely was not going to fall asleep and miss that!

Michael had been pushing me to try to walk down to the cafeteria. I'd been to the cafeteria a few times but usually in a wheelchair. Actually walking to the cafeteria really would have felt impossible and now that I could eat whatever I wanted, it just may be too exciting for me. I won't know how to contain it. We decided to start the trek down the hall to the elevator. All the nurses were waiving and cheering me on. I had my cushy robe and my hospital slippers on. At this point I wasn't really walking, I was scooting, so needless to say it took me a while. Because my vision was blank on the sides from my stroke and my balance was off from not being able to walk, I was slow and I needed help. A lot of help. It was fun. At least it was fun for me. Raegan and Melisa should probably get an award for their patience, but I was smiling and laughing the entire way to the cafeteria. When we walked in, I could smell the food and it was on all sides of me. I felt like a kid walking into Willy Wonka's Chocolate Factory. I couldn't decide. I wanted everything. I grabbed fruit and a turkey sandwich, and they had salads and stir-fry and French fries, and an entire rack of chips. I said, "Melisa, look, chips. Chips." I turned to my left and they were both just standing there laughing at me. I said, "What?" They just kept laughing. It was as if I'd never seen food before. I settled on a turkey sandwich and some fruit. I knew I had my guacamole upstairs and they lectured me about not making myself sick. Melisa decided on a fudge banana bomb. She used to eat them when she was little, and Raegan grabbed some fruit and yogurt. We really were like kids at a slumber party. Nurses would come in and talk with us and watch Kathie Lee and Hoda and we'd all laugh. Michael was so excited when I called him and told him I ate half of my sandwich and almost all the guacamole. If this doesn't kick my kidney into gear, what will?

I spent many, many nights in the hospital. Some were really, really tough. Some were bearable and some I don't even remember, but this night stands out to me. It stood for standing up and fighting. It stood for finding joy in any circumstance. It stood for all the unconditional love and patience everyone had shown me. I fought because of them. I walked and scooted and laughed because of them. And it was the very best guacamole I will ever eat.

Up to this point, I had always felt so weak. Right there at that time, I didn't. I didn't feel weak or helpless or frustrated. I felt normal. We were talking about kids and what had been going on in Shawnee. I felt like a friend and a mom again. Melisa has a way of making you feel important and that you matter. When you are around Melisa, you never feel like she's better than you or that what you're going through isn't normal or that you won't get through it. She pushes you with love and I always knew she'd fight for me to live. And she *did*. She's also the very coolest person I've ever known so just being around her and my girls makes me cooler.

The gift shop was right by the cafeteria and Raegan was pointing at a dress she loved and Missy was laughing at my "scooting" and I just quietly wept. Tonight was a good night.

You see, up to this point, all of our worlds had stopped. My husband and Bauer, Jordan, and Raegan. My mom and dad and family. Michael's family, all of my friends, my cousin Tracy. Their worlds had stopped when mine did. I knew how lucky I was to have people love me. I would spend every day fighting.

I was now "in the moment" of joy and not pain. I was cherishing these moments now.

I forget about the tubes and blood. We watched Kathie Lee and Hoda and then *Duck Dynasty*. I got a little sleep before the nurses came in again to take my blood. I prayed that night and instead of asking for anything I thanked him. I thanked him for my family. I thanked him for Melisa and her guacamole. It sounds silly, but I also thanked him for that turkey sandwich. And that I walked to go buy it. It wasn't just guacamole. It wasn't just a sandwich. It was more of her time. More of her love. A pinch of salt. A pinch of lime and another mile we walked together.

Blair Baluja and Benedict Street

For we walk by faith, not by sight.

—2 Corinthians 5:7 (KJV)

Today I woke up hopeful. This was the day I had been waiting for for weeks. My kidneys had stayed at a normal number for four days now, and I just knew they were gonna let me go home. I woke up and had a feeling that today would be the day.

Dr. Greg opened the door and peeked his head into the room. He walked in and we were all just anxiously staring at him. I started crying softly before he even opened his mouth. He looked at me and said, "How about lunch at Benedict today?" Tears fell down all of our faces. I was finally going home. Michael hit the chair with his fist as if to say, "Yes!"

My family stepped out and Greg sat down. I felt like we'd been through an iron man together, except if we didn't make it to the finish line, I would have died.

He said, "I want to say something to you. I've never seen anyone fight to recover the way you did. I know you have the vision issue but for the most part you are healed. I truly didn't think you were going to *live*."

I couldn't talk.

He continued, "I think you have a guardian angel we both know."

I cried and said, "Yeah, we do."

Nothing else needed to be said. We hugged and he gave me the paperwork to go home. I knew Anne was with us. There were a lot of people with me.

I wasn't just given strength to survive. Greg was given the power to save me. How do I repay him? All these years, we've been through so much together. If you had told me twelve years ago when I met him that he'd save me and my family, I wouldn't be surprised, yet I'd be shocked at the same time. No matter what I do the rest of my life, he'll never know how indebted I am to him.

For the first time, I walked into the bathroom and put real clothes on. No tubes. No IV. No bags. No central lines. Just my weak body. My bones were healed. My heart was strong. My lungs were functioning on their own and my kidneys were getting rid of the toxins. I put on real shoes and sat on the bed waiting to be released. About that time, Dr. Baluja walked in. I threw my hands in the air and said, "Hey! Look at me, you're not used to seeing me with clothes on!" He laughed and I said jokingly, "You know what I mean." Haha.

"You know you're gonna miss me," I said with a smile.

He smiled and said, " Seriously, I will."

Tears started to build up in my eyes and all of these weeks relying on him and talking to him came to mind. It hit me that I wouldn't see him every day and it scared me. I asked, "What if something happens and I need you?" It hit me. I was kind of scared to go home.

"You have my number," he reassured me. "I'm not going anywhere. I want to tell you something," he said with a more serious tone. He took off his glasses and leaned against the back of the chair.

"Julie, I've never witnessed a family, a husband, go through what yours did and handle it with so much grace."

I was softly crying. He continued, "It has been an honor to get to know you and your family. Your kids."

He said, "Julie, I am a man of science, but when I look at you I believe in God. There is no medical reason you should be alive and yet you are *walking*—walking out of this hospital."

My heart was so heavy. I had grown so close to him and depended on him. I didn't know how to get out all I wanted to say, so what came out with tears was, "How do you thank someone for saving your life?"

He replied with distinct denial, "Oh no. It was Dr. Blair. He turned mountains into mole hills, Shawnee doctors and Greg deserve the credit."

I argued back, "It was you too!" More seriously, I said, "Really, I will never be able to repay you for what you've given me."

He said, "Oh, yes, you walking out of here."

Michael, Bauer, Jordan, Raegan, and I packed my room and I waited for the nurses with my release papers.

I will never be able to describe the relationship I have with those two men. I know God brought us together and none of us will ever be the same.

Not Goodbye

Have no anxiety about anything, but in everything by prayer and supplication with thanksgiving, let your request be made known to God. And the peace of God, which passes all understanding, will keep your hearts and your mind in Christ Jesus.

—Philippians 4:6–7 (RSV)

Deep down, I didn't know this day would ever come. When the nurses came in to do my paperwork, I suddenly got kind of scared. How was I going to do this? At the hospital, I was safe. Once out, if something happened to me, I couldn't push a button. If I was in pain, I couldn't call for medicine. How was I going to handle walking and moving around and showering and getting back to being myself all on my own? I had Michael and my mom, my kids, but I had already put them through so much and I knew getting back to everyday, normal life at home was going to be scary. Scary but wonderful. We were going home different people. We were going home a different family.

All the nurses kept coming in to say good-bye. All of them cried and they all told me how proud they were of me. I thought of Sunshine. The last time I saw her, she joked, "You better not be here when I come back from my days off." I knew she'd be proud of me. These people had become like family to me. I thought about what it'd be like to come see them after I'm completely well. I wanted them to see me as a normal person and not as a patient. I thought about them seeing me strong as a parent, a woman. They had all seen me lying in bed weak and needy. I wanted to make them proud and show them who I really was. Then I realized, that's not what these relationships were about. They were paid to give me medicine and they were paid to come in my room and take my blood and check my breathing. What they were not paid to do was care about me and my family, and they did. In ICU, Shelly wasn't paid to cry with me. Traci wasn't paid to sit and talk with my family, not knowing if I'd wake up.

Sunshine didn't have to sit and talk to me. None of them had to bring Michael and my kids cookies they'd baked. I didn't have any idea what it took to be a nurse. And not just a nurse, but a true life saver. You know James, my dialysis guy. He didn't have to talk to me like I mattered. He didn't have to get my crackers when I was nauseated. This experience made me realize so much. You go in and you're in a gown with no makeup, no jewelry. All they know is your name. It doesn't matter what you do for a living or where you live. In that hospital bed, in that gown, you're just like everyone, stripped from all you know that you think matters.

In that bed, to those nurses, you're just like everyone else. All you have is your faith, your family and friends, and the root of who you are on the inside of your soul. The rest means nothing. I guess it took being in a bed with zero ability to move or function or live on my own to realize that. You lay there and your whole life is in their hands. Yes, they are paid to give me breathing treatments and medicine when I'm in pain, but there isn't an amount of money worthy of their compassion. Not any dollar amount that can pay for their empathy and concern. They didn't get paid to care about me and my family. I didn't want to go home and be without them. They all have such a special place in my heart now. I didn't want to forget or lose all of this. Nothing meant more to me than my family. I just wasn't ready to leave these people. I needed them. Michael was so happy. He seemed relieved and scared at the same time. The girls went down to Starbucks to say bye to their new friends. I think everyone we know in town gave them gift cards to Starbucks. It was their favorite place and it was just downstairs. Bauer was ready to go home. He spent hours with my mom and dad and Jordan and Raegan cleaning out his "apartment." From what they described, it was months of food and drinks, probably like his room at home. He enjoyed it but he missed our home. He missed riding his bike and swimming in the neighborhood pool. He wanted everything to be back to normal.

Michael and Raegan had gone home to get the house ready the night before, hoping I'd be released. We'd been gone so long when he walked into the kitchen there was a snake skin on the floor. Of course, he flipped out. He might be Superman, but he doesn't like snakes. Chris and Bryce had come over to see Raegan and help with the house. Little did they know they'd be killing a snake.

Everyone had gone to such great lengths. Not just for me to survive. They fought for me to live. Everyone took care of each other .The nurses took care of me. My family and friends took care of the nurses and doctors. The girls, Bauer, and all of their friends, they all took care of each other. All I had to do was get better. Now I was leaving and I wanted to take care of all of them. I wanted them to know I could.

I decided not to say good-bye to anyone. They say "it takes a village," but I had a football team. They were my new family. I could never say good-bye to Baluja, Greg, Cheema, Kumar, McKinnis, and all my nurses.

These people weren't just a part of this life-changing experience, they were a part of me now. You don't say good-bye to that.

They put all of my stuff on a cart. I sat in a wheelchair and we all started together down the hallway. Wheeling down that hallway, out to the gift shop, and past the cafeteria it was different this time. This time I wasn't going back up that elevator. I was leaving. No one was going to come in at 4:00 AM anymore and take my blood. No one was going to come in and tell me their "awful patient" stories and make me laugh. Dr. Greg and Dr. Baluja and Dr. Cheema weren't going to check on me every morning. I knew I had Michael and my kids. I had my parents and Michael's parents, all my friends and family—yet I was petrified. Was I going to be able to do this?

As we approached the front doors, I asked them to stop. I stood up. I walked outside on my own. Just like Dr. Baluja said I would. The air hit me and I felt a strength and a force go through my body. I was scared to go home because I wouldn't be the same, but I realized, in that moment, that was the point. The fact that we had all changed and we didn't know what was ahead was okay. I was alive and I was different. I didn't have to say good-bye to these people. The nurses and doctors would always be with me. Just like the family I saw in heaven, just like my family when I was with them physically, just like old friends you haven't seen in a while, they are always with us. Gone or here, sick or well, different towns, different lives, we are all connected and no matter what they will always be with me from now on.

We all hugged and the kids and Michael loaded the car. We cried and I got in the car and we drove away. I couldn't stop crying.

I was ready to go home. I wanted to be a wife and mother. I wanted to be in my own bed and sleep on my side and see my dog, Sparky, and wake up with my kids in our own kitchen and our own dishes. At the same time, I felt like we were driving away from such a huge part of my heart. Would I ever see these people again? I wanted to do so many things and come back one day and show them that we won. Show them that what they did for me matters. Show them that they matter and they make a difference. I could never say good-bye, but I was going to try to make them proud. I would accomplish the list I made after I decided it was time to live.

As we drove out of the driveway of the hospital, I was overwhelmed with all that has happened and everything I've learned. God is not finished with me which in a weird way makes it okay that I don't have it all figured out. I have an extraordinary ordinary life and I wouldn't trade it for anyone else's. God is working in our lives every second even if it doesn't feel like it, but it's up to us to do something with it. I didn't have to do something big to do something great. Every struggle has beauty. Every struggle has a lesson. What happens happens *for* us, not *to* us. Life is always going to be difficult at times, but we are not defined by what we have or what we worry about. I truly had to die to learn how to live.

This I Do Know for Sure

Therefore do not worry about tomorrow, for tomorrow will worry about itself.

Each day has enough trouble of its own.

—Matthew 6:34 (NIV)

It's April 2014 now. The flowers are finally blooming after an extremely hard winter. The birds are chirping and every door in my house is open so the fresh air can blow through the entire house. My body is healed. My lungs are weak but working. My vision blocked and blurry, but for the most part, I'm healthy. Heart is beating. Kidneys are strong. Blood is flowing through my heart. Even my hand has almost all function back. My ring is still sliced open and I have a few scars, but unless you know what happened, you wouldn't be able to tell by looking at me. But I was different. You wouldn't know my entire life stopped and by the grace of God, I was able to come back and find it. To stand in the middle of something so horrifying and see the light. Not the darkness. That's where the beauty of losing part of my vision lies. The loss of vision was a chance to choose what I wanted to see.

I never could have expected what happened. You don't make your list out for the week and write:

Monday-dance
Tuesday-baseball
Wednesday-soccer
Thursday-die

The good thing is love is stronger than our mistakes and prayer is stronger than we are.

Everyone has struggles.

Everyone has a story.

This is my story. There are a lot of stories out there—stories of faith and hope, family and love, mistakes and regret, and death. I decided to tell mine. It is my truth the way it happened. I hope it is embraced. I hope it helps people with their own story, helps you look at your life and make changes for what matters to you.

This is not about me. It is about God working through me. It is about that light that pulled me back to where I belonged—the light that guided me to find those minutes I'd lost, my body back to my soul, my soul back to my self.

The voices of people I'd loved. The memories that made me who I am. Everything came together that day so God would show me how to live. I hope my story makes a difference. It is told to give hope and show faith where there is none. It is meant to find love and compassion for those who have given up. It is meant to show there is more than medicine to healing. I tell it to wake you up. I tell it so you'll hold on to your children, smile and laugh with them. Tell the person you love how you feel before you can't. I tell it so you'll get in your car, roll down the windows, and drive. Turn the music up and sing. Breathe in the air. Remember who you wanted to be, but don't forget who you are.

Go enjoy your life. Be happy. Give your struggle and your regrets to God and start over. Go soak in people and music instead of your phone and computer.

Dance. Work. Have a purpose and *go live*. Most importantly, don't forget to take God with you when you go.

In the future, I'll remember what happened with a sense of clarity. I'll know what's important with a sense of love and family. I'll know what matters and how to make a difference now, and in the end, I'll look at the clouds from the passenger seat and remember where I've been. This I know for sure.

The Story of the Painting

My grace is sufficient for you, for my power is made perfect in weakness.

—2 Corinthians 12:9 (NIV)

In April 2013, my very talented friend, Paula, had an art show. She had many beautiful paintings and drawings. I went initially to support my friend and enjoy the company of many other friends. I started to look for a painting. I thought if I had a peaceful painting of calm waters to look at in the morning, my recurring dream of drowning would maybe go away. I talked to Paula for a while about it, and we looked around, but she didn't really have anything already finished that was close to what I was looking to buy. She asked me questions of what I was really wanting and said she would try to get it started, and she would let me know. After I got out of the hospital, Paula and Rae Ann brought me dinner one night. Much time passed since we'd talked about the painting. Paula knew I was writing a book and asked if she could paint me the picture I had asked for it to go with it.

I was so honored. Those paintings take so much work and time. When she brought the painting over to my house, I couldn't believe it. It was so much like what I had envisioned, and it had *two* canoes in the center. I had never shared with her there were *two* canoes. I was humbled when I looked at it and grateful to have her as my friend. I look at it every day, and it does give me peace. It has become a great part of my story.

Grandpa and me

Tea Party with my dad

My Grandpa

My family at Santa Monica Pier

Michael's family

Michael and I

Raegan, Bauer and Jordan: Christmas 2004

The girls with Michael's parents:
Mike and Debi Brittain

My mom and dad:
Mike and Betty Presley

Grandma, Tracy, and
my Aunt Judy

My cousin Brent, he was the
one that cut my ring off while
I was coding

Michael's siblings: Kim, Michael, Jennifer, and Jason

My siblings: Me, Allyson, and Pat

Bauer and Michael

Jordan, Me, and Raegan,
one week before I died

Jordan, Bauer, and Raegan;
Shawnee football picture

Bauer doing what he
loves the most

Jordan and Raegan

Brook, Danielle, Samantha,
April, and Amy. Childhood friends

Me and my crazy friend Summer

Me and Angie

My Melissa

The Blair family

Nicki, my highschool friend that helped save my life

Waking up in New Mexico

Anne

"Asleep"

Play for Julie

Michael texting me while I was "asleep"

Prayers sent from Jordan and Raegan's friends

Bauer and Langston asleep
at the hospital, waiting for
me to wake up

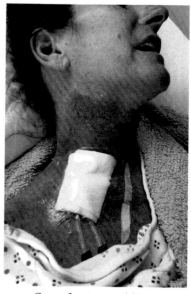

One of my central lines

My healing hand

Melissa's perfect guacamole

Independence Day

Fireworks

Jesus as I saw him.

Peace

My family finally taking me home

Michael, Cammie, Me, Kelli—meeting Cammie
after she helped save my life

Cammie, Sylvia, Me and Kelli

Me and my lunch crew—April, Kim, Melissa,
Angie, Me, Shai, and Rachael

My Blair family: Alex, Jordan, Erin,
Raegan, Jennifer, and Me

Terry, Me, and Jennifer

Carol and Rachel

Dr. Blair and Dr. Baluja. My lifesavers! Literally.

Kim, Renee, and Me

Terrie and Me

Tonya and Taylor

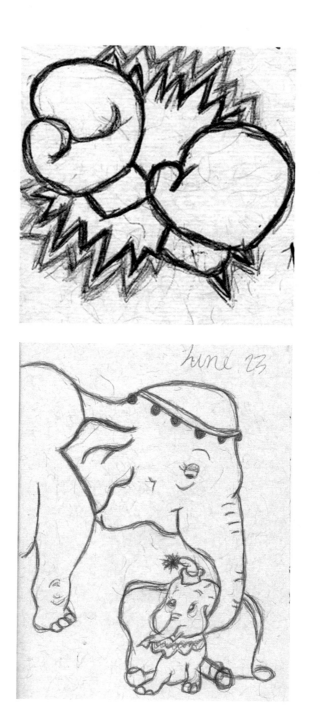